*Jewish
Folklore
and
Legend*

JEWISH FOLKLORE AND LEGEND

David Goldstein

HAMLYN

LONDON · NEW YORK · SYDNEY · TORONTO

Published by
The Hamlyn Publishing Group Limited
London · New York · Sydney · Toronto
Astronaut House, Feltham, Middlesex, England

© Copyright David Goldstein 1980
ISBN 0 600 36365 1

Phototypeset in England by Tradespools Limited,
Frome, Somerset
Printed and bound in Great Britain by
R. J. Acford Ltd., Industrial Estate, Chichester, Sussex

Contents

INTRODUCTION

I T WAS the custom in some medieval Jewish communities for a
child to have his first taste of the Torah by actually eating some
selected Biblical verses. The Hebrew letters of Scripture would
be smeared in honey on a slate, and the child would lick them
avidly, thus fulfilling the verses: 'How sweet are your words to my
taste, sweeter than honey to my mouth' (Psalm 119:103), and '[The
Scroll] was in my mouth like honey in sweetness' (Ezekiel 3:3).

The Torah in its narrowest sense signifies the Pentateuch,
otherwise known as the Five Books of Moses, the first part of the
Hebrew Bible. In its wider sense, however, it denotes also all the
ramifications of the Pentateuch – the commentaries that the rabbis
wrote upon it, the laws that are derived from it, the elaborations of
the narrative portions – in fact, practically the whole of Jewish
religious literature can be subsumed under the all-embracing title of
Torah. Since this Torah derives ultimately from God, there can be
for the Jew no more worthy object of study. 'Turn it over and over
again, for everything is in it. Contemplate it and grow old and grey
over it, and do not digress from it, for you can have no better rule
than [the Torah]' (*Mishnah Avot* 5:22).

One can see therefore that the usual translation of the word
'Torah' as 'Law' is inadequate. Its basic meaning is rather 'teaching'
or 'instruction'. But it is even more than the solid and revered bed-
rock of Jewish faith. It is also an object of love. The *Sefer Torah*
(Scroll of the Torah) from which portions are read weekly in the
synagogue is a Jewish community's most treasured possession. At
times it becomes almost a person, as when on the Festival of
Rejoicing in the Torah (*Simhat Torah*) a Jew takes the scroll in his
arms and dances with it in joyful abandon; or when it is counted as
one of the *minyan*, the quorum of ten needed for the recitation of
certain statutory prayers.

The Torah is beloved, of course, not for its own physical nature, but for its sacred contents. The laws, interpreted as they have been down the ages in countless commentaries, codified, and still subject to minute dissection and discussion, are incumbent on every observant Jew. And the Biblical narratives have been analysed, explained and elaborated to such an extent that a Jew 'of the old school' can hardly distinguish between what Scripture actually says and what later expositors have understood it to say. The legal content of the Torah is known as *halakhah*, while the narratives form the basis of *aggadah*. Aggadah simply means 'telling', and this 'telling' can cover practically any aspect of human life. It can fill in the details of a Biblical story, reconcile apparent contradictions, answer questions (and pose them too!), incorporate fables from other sources, make moral deductions, add contemporary historical allusions, discuss relevant theological topics, indulge in biographical anecdotes, and it can even make remarks of a legal character which properly belong to the realm of halakhah. The aggadah can be pithy and opaque. It can also ramble, moving from one story to another, and from one theme to another, until the reader is in danger of forgetting the original starting-point. The aggadah can be serious and philosophically profound, and at the next moment lend itself to irrational fantasies, or appear irreverently comic.

The story in Genesis of how Cain killed Abel is well known. But have you ever thought of how they disposed of the body, 'for they did not know what to do with Abel since they had no experience of burial? Then a raven appeared who had been bereaved of one of his companions. He took the dead bird, and dug a hole in the ground and buried it. Adam saw this and said: "I shall do the same as the raven." He took Abel's corpse, dug a hole in the ground and buried it' (*Pirke de-Rabbi Eliezer* 21). This is a simple example of how the aggadah supplies 'missing' information.

The Book of Jonah contains a fascinating and moving moral tale in its own right. It does not really require much explanation. But the aggadah wants to tell us more about the righteous and sin-fearing character of the mariners with whom Jonah had embarked. So it says that at first they were reluctant to throw Jonah into the waves. They thought they would see if a semi-immersion would do, and they put Jonah overboard and held him in the water up to his waist. And sure enough, the storm stopped. But when they pulled him in again, the storm recommenced. The same thing happened when they ducked him up to his neck. So they had no alternative but to cast him completely into the sea. The same work then links the Jonah story to events that according to Jewish legend will take place at the end of time. The fish that swallowed Jonah warns him that it is about to be eaten by Leviathan, the great monster of the deep. 'Take me to him,' says Jonah. Jonah confronts Leviathan and tells him that in the days to come he, Jonah, will catch him and drag him out of the sea and feed his flesh to the righteous in paradise. Leviathan takes fright and swims away. The fish in gratitude for Jonah's intercession spews him out on to the dry land. (*Pirke de-Rabbi Eliezer* 10.)

The aggadah contains hundreds upon hundreds of legends and fables, most of which serve to illustrate in some way the Scriptural text, although others are quite independent of it and are attached because they have a moral or historical message, or simply because the stories are too good to be left out! There are many collections of aggadic material. The oldest of them evolved from the expositions of the Bible given by rabbis in the synagogues of Palestine from the earliest centuries CE.* Such an exposition is called *midrash* (plural, *midrashim*), from a verbal root meaning 'to seek or enquire'. As the prescribed weekly section was read from the Torah, the rabbi would elucidate and elaborate it for the edification and delight of the community. The point of origin of the interpretation is the text itself. Alternatively, ideas may generate themselves in the minds of the expositors who then seek to find proof-texts for them in the words of Scripture. Midrash is therefore a two-way exercise: it is both inspiration and justification.

To deliver oneself of a midrash is both an act of piety and a means of instruction. It often requires great ingenuity in handling the Hebrew text. One might note, for example, how a word used in one place in the Bible occurs in exactly the same form in only one other place, and draw a moral or theological conclusion from the parallel. Even an idiosyncratic spelling can give rise to a story. The Torah is an inexhaustible supply of wisdom, and therefore every generation can find in it something fresh and original. A rabbi to this day feels himself well pleased if he can discover a *hiddush* (something new) in

*CE = Christian Era (i.e. AD); BCE = Before the Christian Era (i.e. BC).

the Torah that no one before has perceived. The use of exacting textual observation in the creation of a moral-theological point can be seen in a midrash on Exodus 12:23: '"The Lord will pass through to smite the Egyptians." We find that God judged the generation of the Flood while seated, since Scripture says "The Lord sat enthroned at the Flood" [Psalm 29:10]. But he judged the Egyptians as he passed through . . . In the days to come, however, God will stand up when he judges the world, for Scripture says "His feet shall stand in that day" [Zechariah 14:4]. Future generations will say: "If God judged the generation of the Flood while seated, and yet annihilated them; and if he slew the Egyptian first-born, while passing through; who will be able to endure in the days to come when God will actually stand to judge the world?" . . . But why will he stand? In response to the cries of the poor, as Scripture says "For the oppression of the poor, for the sighing of the needy, now will I arise, saith the Lord" [Psalm 12:6]'. (*Exodus Rabbah* 17:4.)

Many of the stories in midrashic literature did not, however, originate from the study of the text itself. They were popular folk-tales dealing with Biblical themes or personalities, and they were adopted by the Jewish teachers in synagogues and schools and incorporated into midrashic collections. Occasionally we find there legends which are common to the people in general, but which were transmuted, with appropriate changes, into specifically Jewish stories and applied to Biblical situations. Some of the tales concerning the creation are of this type, as also a few of the accounts of contests between Solomon and the prince of the demons. Many of the motifs are common to more than one folk-culture, and it is notoriously difficult to trace a chronological or geographical chain of transmission.

On the other hand, midrashic interpretations found their way into European folklore, sometimes through the literature of Judaism's two daughter religions: Christianity and Islam. Early Christian literature is, of course, very close in nature to Jewish texts, and it is not surprising to find both in the Gospels and in the writings of the Church Fathers elaborations of Scripture which can be paralleled in Jewish sources. Thus, for example, the Jewish idea of Elijah as a forerunner of the Messiah occurs in Luke 1:17.

The Koran displays many examples of the influence of midrash. Mahommed gained much of his knowledge of the Bible and of

Judaism from Jewish sages in his immediate environment, and they would naturally embellish the Biblical narratives in the traditional midrashic way. There is, however, a major difference in the approach of the two religions to the Hebrew Scriptures. To the Muslims the patriarchs are invariably perfect human beings, consistently and unimpeachably righteous in their moral conduct. They even accused the rabbis of tampering with the text of the Bible, and interpolating episodes which reveal the patriarchs in a less than perfect light. For the Jews, however, the heroes of the Scriptural narrative are fallible human beings, struggling to overcome their failings in the service of the one God, whose pre-eminence and sovereignty they were the first to recognise. No man is perfect. Indeed, it is this more realistic attitude of the Jewish tradition that generated much of the midrashic material.

Abraham, Isaac, Jacob, Moses, Aaron, Joshua are, of course, models of God-fearing piety and righteousness. But they are also in Jewish eyes people of flesh and blood, with many of the foibles and failings that characterise the rest of humanity. That is why Jews can enjoy a personal, almost familiar, relationship with these revered sages of the past. They can be treated as friends as well as paragons of virtue. The ultimate in the combination of these two elements is seen in Jewish mysticism (kabbalah), in which the patriarchs are symbols of different aspects of the deity, and therefore logically remote from everyday human perception. But they are also so familiar to the kabbalist that he can invite them to be his guests (*ushpizin*) and to visit his *sukkah* (temporary dwelling) during the Festival of Tabernacles.

How seriously are we to take the aggadah? Were the stories and legends meant to be believed literally, or are they no more than artistic or didactic embroideries on Biblical themes? No single answer can be given to these questions. It is clear that some of the more fantastic stories, such as those concerning the giant Og, were intended to excite the reader's or listener's imagination, and must be regarded very much as we regard the legends surrounding King Arthur's court. On the other hand, stories concerning the demonic world may very well have been taken at their face value. Even if some of them may appear to us today to belong to the realm of primitive fear and superstition, they probably originally reflected real beliefs, and when they became part of the kabbalist's world picture from the twelfth century onwards they impinged on his everyday life and affected his method of performing ritual acts.

It would not be accurate, however, to say that midrashic literature is a collection of Jewish mythology. Myths seek primarily to explain major cosmic processes, and although the Jews were undoubtedly influenced by ancient Near Eastern mythologies they rewrote them in such a way as to transform them into stories which illustrated the power of the one God, the Creator of the Universe. Mythology did, however, reassert itself in Jewish mysticism, where cosmic forces, though still subservient to the Godhead, assumed the role of independent powers that had influence on terrestrial life.

The stories in the aggadah may be appreciated primarily for their entertainment value. But most of them do contain basic moral and theological ideas. It is important to recognise that the rabbis of the Mishnaic and Talmudic period, that is, in the first six centuries CE, did not write moral or theological treatises. Their views on such matters as reward and punishment, the after-life, the nature and attributes of God, the place of Israel in the divine scheme, have to be gleaned from comments scattered over the vast range of rabbinic literature – both from the aggadah and from legal discussions. They therefore often present us with contradictory statements, or ideas that are the preserve of one individual rabbi and not shared by his companions. The stories they told, whether connected with Biblical themes or not, were a vehicle for the expression of these basic religious concepts.

The aggadah, consequently, could not have the binding force of halakhah. The latter, since it instructed the Jews how to act, had to be obeyed so that unity could be imposed on what would be otherwise disparate systems of religious practice. But the aggadah, which was more spiritual than practical in nature, belonging to the realm of faith rather than action, could command no such universal commitment. One either believed the stories or not, and one was at liberty to create one's own midrash, or add to the interpretations of others. No sanctions could be imposed on the cerebrations of the human mind, as long as they did not manifest themselves in action.

We may conclude, therefore, that aggadah was intended primarily to draw the Jew nearer to the sacred text of Scripture by planting within his heart, through story and interpretation, a love of the personalities of the Bible, a greater realisation of the nature, ways and teaching of God, and a deeper understanding of the destiny of Israel.

It is clear from what follows that I have been constrained by availability of space to select drastically from an enormous range of material. I have deliberately omitted the vast number of legends and stories that do not impinge directly on Biblical motifs. I have not therefore drawn upon the Hasidic corpus, which is mainly concerned with the dicta of, and legends concerning the Hasidic rabbis; nor have I chosen tales about the individual rabbis of *Mishnah* and *Talmud*, except in so far as they incorporate themes connected with the Bible. I have also tried to present those stories which lend themselves most readily to pictorial illustration.

Source references are given in the text. They include the various collections of midrashim; the Jerusalem and the Babylonian Talmuds; the *Targumim*, (Aramaic translations of Biblical books, often containing midrashic elements); medieval Bible commentaries; and a few secondary sources from which I have drawn, for example, Muslim parallels. References to the Bible are to the Hebrew editions, and chapter and verse numbers do not always tally with the English translations.

A few words about the major sources used will help to put the material in a chronological framework. The two *Talmudim* are both expansions of the *Mishnah*, a corpus of Jewish law which was compiled by Rabbi Judah the Prince in about 200 CE. The Jerusalem (otherwise known as the Palestinian) Talmud was written in Palestine, and reached its present form by the mid-fifth century. The Babylonian Talmud is both more extensive and more authoritative. It was finished in Babylonia, modern Iraq, by the mid-sixth century, and is cited by its various tractates, e.g. *Sanhedrin*, *Megillah*, *Berakhot*, etc.

The most basic collection of midrashim is the *Midrash Rabbah*, or Great Midrash. It is a midrash on the Pentateuch, and on the five so-called *megillot*, comprising the Song of Songs, Ruth, Lamentations, Ecclesiastes, and Esther. Its oldest section, that on Genesis, goes back to the fifth century CE, but additions were made over a long period of time, and the complete work reached its present form not earlier than 1100.

The *Pirke de-Rabbi Eliezer* (Chapters of Rabbi Eliezer) is a midrashic work on Genesis and parts of Exodus and Numbers, and was ascribed to the first century CE Rabbi Eliezer ben Hyrcanus. But it was probably written in Palestine in the eighth century.

The main work of kabbalah is the *Zohar* (Splendour), which although attributed to Rabbi Simeon ben Yohai of the second century CE did not appear until the end of the thirteenth century in Spain, and was probably compiled there by Rabbi Moses de Leon.

Very often a particular story occurs in more than one source, and is expanded, or shortened, or changed in some way from one source to another. This is to be expected in the transmission of legend which was partly oral in character. The references do not denote necessarily the earliest source, but the one which has served as the basis for the version of the story I give.

CREATION

THE DETAILS of the creation story (or, rather, stories) that we find in the Bible may be profitably compared with accounts in the mythologies of the ancient Near Eastern world. Man's imagination created stories in order to explain the natural phenomena which surrounded him, forces which were stronger than him, and upon which he depended for his very existence. The heat of the sun, the fructifying power of the rain, the destructiveness of the storm-wind, the threatening expanse of the sea, and the never-ending cycle of life and decay, these were some of the main elements which filled him with dread and also with wonder. He was at their mercy. By endowing them with a personality which was similar but in every way superior to his own he was able to effect a means of communication with them. He could talk to them, plead with them, make promises to them, and engage in a series of ritual acts which could control or at least influence them. It is possible, of course, that ritual preceded mythology, that man first made obeisance before the forces of nature, and then became conscious of 'events' in the life of these forces. Be that as it may, the whole natural world seemed to man to be endowed with divinity. Every part of it had its own life, and it had a relationship – of dependence, superiority, hostility or friendship – with other parts. Water, fire, and the wind; the earth, sun, moon, and stars; mountains, springs and groves, formed the sacred environment in which man lived, worked and bred.

The mythologies which grew up around these phenomena explained their origins and the functions they performed in the whole natural drama, in which man played but a small and generally insignificant part. The ancient gods of sea and sky, of fire and fertility, were at times locked in divine combat, and at others united in divine love, and the experiences 'in heaven' had a direct effect on the terrestrial sphere, and thus on man. Indeed, on occasions, and particularly in later Greek mythology, man himself was called upon to play an active role in the affairs of the gods. The interdependence of the human and the divine, which is such a prominent feature of religion, can thus be said to originate in mythology.

In the pages that follow we shall be able to find parallels in Near Eastern mythology for Biblical stories or for specific features in those stories. However, it is important to realise that the mythological content of the Biblical narratives themselves is very weak. The underlying myths have undergone a transformation which has practically deprived them altogether of their mythical element. The stories have been recast or retold in such a way that we sometimes have to exercise considerable ingenuity to find the underlying mythological idea. What we have before us in the early chapters of Genesis is no less than a process of demythologisation.

The change in religious approach is absolutely fundamental and perfectly clear. The basic elements of nature have been robbed of their divinity. The heavenly spheres are no longer gods. The wind and the rain have no divine independence. They are all subservient to one God. This God has no rivals, and his existence is accepted as a fact beyond both dispute and enquiry. Preoccupation with the origin of the divine powers, a major theme of ancient mythology, is completely absent from the Biblical narrative. It was enough simply to state 'God said', 'God saw'. Indeed, one might say that the most significant influence of myth in the Biblical presentation of God is the attribution to him of human actions, and this remains a problem which has exercised the minds of all Western theologians. For how can one talk of God at all without using the terms of speech which are common to us?

There are two main accounts in the Bible of the creation of the world. They are different in style and in content, but they are not really contradictory. The second account beginning with Genesis 2:4 is more dramatic and picturesque, and is concerned principally with Adam, the first man, and God's relationship with him. The first account (which immediately precedes the second) is strictly chronological in style, and is more analytic and abstract; one might even say more 'scientific'. Here too man is presented as the crown of creation, the master of the animal and vegetable world, but the account concludes not with man but with a description of the first

Sabbath, and it is likely that this story of creation in six days was intended to be a justification of the institution and observance of the Sabbath.

This ordered presentation of the divine creative process is meant to portray with complete clarity and certitude the way in which God imposed order on chaos. The Bible does not speak of *creatio ex nihilo*: 'The act of creation consisted in bringing order out of chaos, not of bringing matter into existence out of nothing.'* The first words of the Bible should properly be rendered 'When God began to create heaven and earth, the earth was a formless waste.' A significant feature of this chaos was the existence of a turbulent and unconstrained watery deep (Hebrew, *tehom*).

The Lower Waters

The creation story in the Babylonian epic *Enuma Elish* also speaks of the very beginning when Tiamat, the ocean of salt water, united with Apsu, the ocean of sweet water, to bring forth all the gods. The primal existence of water is a common motif in many ancient mythologies, in some of which the god or goddess of the sea, perhaps in the form of a great watery serpent, has to be overcome by a more beneficent power before the world as we know it could come into being. Only remnants of this idea remain in the Bible in the shape of the monster Leviathan and it is worth noting that Genesis 1:21 states unequivocally that 'God created the great sea-monsters' as if to scotch the idea that these monsters had any part to play in the divine cosmogony. They like all other creatures are, and always were, subservient to him.

The primal nature of water is also evident in the Bible, in the second account of creation, where we read that before the appearance of vegetation, and before there was any rain 'an *ed* went up from the earth and watered the whole face of the ground' (Genesis 2:6). *Ed* is traditionally translated 'mist' but it almost certainly means an upsurge of water. Speiser (p. 14) translates 'A flow would well up from the ground' while the *New English Bible* renders 'A flood used to rise out of the earth'. This subterranean water made a contribution to the Flood in the time of Noah: 'all the springs of the

*Hooke, *Middle Eastern Mythology*, p. 109.

great abyss [*tehom*] broke through' (Genesis 7:11).

In order to make the world as it now appears God had to keep these waters in check. He divided them horizontally, stretching out over them a *rakia*, which denotes a sheet of beaten ,metal, a 'firmament', and he then gathered the water below the *rakia* into specific areas so that the dry land could appear between them. He 'set the springs of ocean firm in their place' and 'prescribed limits for the sea' (Proverbs 8:28–9).

This theme represents the later mythological one of the gods' contest with and ultimate subjugation of the 'lower waters'. And although in the Bible we hear only faint echoes of this struggle, in later Jewish literature it comes to the fore again.

Patai in his *Man and Temple* (p. 62 ff) points out that in some midrashim the lower waters are considered to be female and the upper waters male. It is their constant desire to unite which threatens universal devastation. God, therefore, had to separate them.

In the *Jerusalem Talmud* there is a story of how David was one day digging the foundations of the Temple. He penetrated more than two thousand feet below the surface of the earth, and he came across a shard. David bent down to lift the shard, but it cried out and advised him not to. 'Why not?' said David. 'Because,' replied the shard, 'I cover the abyss.' The shard goes on to say that God had placed it there when he proclaimed at Sinai, 'I am the Lord thy God.' Other versions say that the shard had been there since the creation of the world. David, however, took no notice. He lifted the shard, and the waters began to rise from the abyss, threatening to engulf the whole earth. David knew that it would not help simply to throw the shard back into the water, since it might sink without reaching the exact spot from which it came. He appealed for help from those around him. Ahitophel came forward and had the divine name inscribed on the shard. The shard was thrown into the abyss and the waters began to subside. In fact they sank so quickly that David was afraid the earth might become entirely dry and wither away. So he composed the fifteen Psalms entitled *Song of Ascents*, to encourage the water to rise again to an acceptable level (*J. Talmud Sanhedrin* 10, 29a). The *Zohar* (II, 91b) tells us that man's moral conduct has an influence on the shard's ability to restrain 'the lower waters'. Whenever a man swears falsely by God's name, the letters of that name on the shard disappear, and the waters burst out to destroy the world. God has therefore put the angel Yazriel in charge of the shard. This angel has in his keeping the seventy graving tools and with these he ensures that the letters of the divine name are constantly replaced on the shard, thus saving the world. In kabbalah, the power of evil, the 'other side', otherwise designated as the serpent, has his abode in 'the crevices of the great deep' (*tehom rabba*). The rising of the lower waters is therefore a continual threat to the existence of the world.

Light

It was not only the unruly waters that God needed to control. The deeps were covered by 'thick darkness'. And the very first divine act was the creation of light. Yet there is a problem here if the words of Scripture are to be interpreted literally, because the source of light, the sun and moon, were not created until the fourth day. The midrash solves the difficulty by supposing that the light created on the first day was not the light we know on earth, but a special supernal light, reserved for heavenly use only. It is the light that is stored up for the pious and the good, the 'light that is sown for the righteous' (Psalm 97:11). As such it became the object of all mystic contemplation and endeavour. It is noteworthy, however, that unlike some ancient myths, that of Prometheus being the most well known, there is no hint in the Biblical story that God was ever jealous of his light, or attempted to deny mankind the ability to make it himself. The forbidden area, as we shall see, was 'knowledge of good and evil' and consequent immortality.

God created the two lights, 'the greater light' and 'the lesser light', that is, the sun and moon, to rule respectively over the day and the night. Once more, the plain, direct statements of Scripture rule out any possibility of these heavenly bodies being credited with an independent power of their own. Their power is subject to the suzerainty of their Creator. It was necessary to state such irrefutable beliefs, because there were times when the Jews did fall to worshipping celestial beings, as is evidenced by prophetic denunciations of the practice, in Jeremiah for example, who condemns the vows that the people made 'to the queen of heaven', and libations that were poured out to her (44:15 ff). Indeed, small figures of

Astarte, the moon-goddess, the queen of heaven, are among the most common images found by archaeologists, even on sites which must have been occupied by Jews.

The fascination of the moon reasserted itself in Jewish tradition at a much later date, in the kabbalistic view of the universe, which was dominated by the mystic world of the *sefirot*. According to the *Zohar*, the thirteenth-century foundation work of Jewish mysticism, the moon is a symbol of the *Shekhinah* (divine presence), that aspect of the divinity which is the most closely involved with the world. The Shekhinah is female and is the partner of *Tiferet*, symbolised by the sun, from whom she receives influence and power, just as the moon possesses only reflected light from the sun, without having any light of its own. For the kabbalist, the fulfilment of the commandments, and in particular the recital of prayers, cannot be directed towards the true essence of God who is far beyond human perception and understanding. The mystic concentrates on the Shekhinah and tries by his good deeds to 'elevate' her towards her 'husband' Tiferet, and thus initiate a process of harmony in the upper worlds.

The lower world in which we live has its counterpart in the upper, divine world. The sun, moon and stars, the Temple, the patriarchs, the people of Israel – are all patterned on the supernal types in the world above. And anything that happens in this world has an effect, either beneficial or detrimental, on the corresponding feature in the upper world. Although the full-detailed ramifications of this idea are not spelled out until the medieval period, its seeds were sown in the rabbinic interpretation of the creation story which we find in the *Talmud* and midrash. And the rabbis themselves may well have been influenced by the Platonic theory of the existence of ideal abstract types in 'heaven', which have their concrete parallel images on earth.

Torah and Creation

The bare bones of the creation story as narrated in the first chapter of Genesis were filled out by later Jewish tradition. The biblical account assigns no place, for example, to the Torah in the creative scheme. And yet for the rabbis the Torah, God's teaching, revealed to man on Sinai, was his supreme gift. It was natural to presume, therefore, that it was among the first things to be created. According to one tradition God actually created the Torah first, and then consulted it before creating the world. This was often adduced as an interpretation of Proverbs 3:19, 'The Lord by wisdom founded the earth; by understanding he established the heavens' ('wisdom' and 'understanding' being synonymous with Torah); and especially of 8:22, 'The Lord made me [i.e. wisdom] as the beginning of his way, the first of his works of old. I was set up from everlasting, from the beginning. . . .' The Torah then became personalised as a kind of artisan, a medium by which the creation of the world was set in motion, and the whole creative process planned. In this sense it may be seen as the Logos, or the divine word.

Connected with the idea that the Torah was present at God's side at the creation is the view that the letters of the Hebrew alphabet were themselves instrumental in the formation of the world. This view is most directly put at the beginning of the *Sefer Yezirah* (The Book of Formation), which was attributed to the patriarch, Abraham, but is by an unknown author from the third (?) century CE. It states there that the world was created by the twenty-two letters of the Hebrew alphabet and the ten numbers, which together form the thirty-two paths of understanding.

A delightful midrash tells the story of how all the letters of the alphabet vied with each other for the honour of being the first to be written in the Torah. The claim of each was examined and rejected until the letter *Beth* presented itself. Because she begins the word *barukh* (blessed) and is therefore the means by which the whole of mankind bless and praise God she was selected. So the Bible begins with the Hebrew word *bereshit* (in the beginning). The first letter of the alphabet *alef* was extremely humble and did not press her claim at all, and for this God rewarded her by putting her at the very beginning of the Ten Commandments in the word *Anokhi* (I).

Angels

The origin of the angelic beings is not systematically presented in Jewish tradition. Their creation, nature and function are variously portrayed in the different stages of Jewish religious development and in the literature produced by each stage.

Angels do not figure in the Biblical creation story at all. God himself and alone is in charge. They do make an appearance in later parts of the scriptural narrative, but their nature is not defined. The Hebrew word usually translated 'angel' is *malakh*, which means simply 'messenger' (as does the Greek rendering *angelos*). Malakh is used in the Bible of both human and superhuman beings. Jacob's adversary at Penuel (Genesis 32:25 ff) is described as 'a man', and as 'God', but Hosea in his reference to the struggle calls him a malakh (Hosea 12:5). The prophet known by the name 'Malachi' was simply designated thereby as 'my messenger'. The being who announced the forthcoming birth of Samson to Manoah's wife (Judges 13:2 ff) is called an 'angel [malakh] of the Lord', but when she tells the story to her husband she says, 'A man of God came to me.' This, however, may be because she did not recognise him as an angel. The narration, in fact, says specifically of Manoah that he 'did not know that he was the angel of the Lord'. It was only when the angel 'ascended in the flame of the altar' that they realised who he really was. In the famous story of Balaam's ass (Numbers 22:21 ff), the angel with a sword in his hand appears to the ass but is invisible to Balaam. Only in the Book of Daniel, which is the youngest of the Biblical books, are actual names given to angels. There we read of Gabriel and Michael.

Angels are not described in any physical detail in the Bible, except in so far as they appear in human form. Isaiah sees a great vision of the seraphim in the Temple (Isaiah 6:2). They were part of God's retinue, and were it seems creatures of fire (*saraph* means 'burn'), but they were also winged. 'Each one had six wings: with two he covered his face, with two he covered his feet, and with two he flew.' But Isaiah does not identify the seraphim with angels. Nor are the cherubim to be so identified. These were sphinx-like creatures with human heads, the bodies of a lion, and wings. They are mentioned as providing the base for the divine throne in the sanctuary. The great guardians of the gateways of Assyrian Nineveh were probably quite like the cherubim in form. The description that Ezekiel gives of his vision of the chariot-throne of God is full of complex images: 'they had the likeness of a man. Each one had four faces, and each one had four wings, and their feet were straight feet; and the sole of their feet was like the sole of a calf's foot; and they sparkled like the colour of burnished brass' (Ezekiel 1:5 ff). But here again they are not identified as 'angels'.

Job 1:6 and 2:1 speaks of 'the sons of God' who come 'to present themselves before the Lord'. Among them is one called *satan*, the adversary, who appears again in a vision that is revealed to Zechariah by an angel (Zechariah 3:1 ff). The 'sons of God' are also the subject of an episode narrated in Genesis 6:1 ff (see p. 25) but what their true nature and purpose were is not clear.

We may suggest two hypotheses about this wealth of unsystematised material concerning superhuman beings: either there was no clearly formed view of the celestial divine entourage, its hierarchy and nomenclature; or there was such a view that was so well known to their audience that the Biblical writers did not need to spell it out. One thing is certain, however, and that is that all these powers are subject to the authority of God, and are not his rivals.

In post-biblical Jewish writing angels assume a much larger and more important role. This is especially so of those books which have an eschatological theme, such as the First Book of Enoch. There we encounter four angels by name, Michael, Gabriel, Raphael and Phanuel, who are portrayed as 'angels of the presence'. In rabbinic literature the place of Phanuel is taken by Uriel. The writings of the Dead Sea sect found at Qumran also contain many references to angels and other celestial beings involved in the struggle at the end of time: the war between the sons of light and the sons of darkness.

There are many references to angels in Talmudic and midrashic literature. According to one view they were formed on the second day of creation, and not on the first, so that men should not believe that they were responsible for the existence of heaven and earth (*Genesis Rabba* 1:3; 3:8), and according to another they were created with the birds on the fifth day. There is a hierarchy of ten stages, at the top being the four angels of the presence already mentioned. Every nation in the world (in the rabbinic view there were seventy in all) has its own prince in the celestial sphere, who looks after its interests. When the nation suffers, the prince suffers too.

Sometimes this is expressed in astrological terms, every nation being under the jurisdiction and guidance of one specific planet or star. The exception is Israel. *En mazzal le-Yisrael*: 'Israel has no presiding star', God himself being solely responsible for Israel's destiny (*Shabbat* 156a). (*Mazzal*, 'planet', came gradually to mean 'luck'; hence the congratulatory phrase *mazzal tov*, 'good luck'.)

One of the angels' main tasks is to praise God. Some are created only for a moment, utter their praises and then vanish. There are several statements to the effect that the recital of praises in heaven depends on the praising of God by human beings on earth. The angels wait for the Jews below to say their prayers. This imposes a great responsibility on the human worshipper (*Hullin* 91a). When the angels protested at this state of affairs God reprimanded them saying that in one respect human beings were their superiors in that they had to overcome their evil inclinations by which angels were not troubled. There was another famous occasion on which the praising angels incurred the divine displeasure. This was when they began to heap eulogies upon the Almighty at his miraculous feat at the Red Sea,* where the Egyptians were drowned. God stopped them, saying, 'It is My creatures who are drowning. How dare you sing?' (*Sanhedrin* 39b).

In rabbinic literature the angels retain their original significance as the messengers of the divine. God used them with admirable economy. 'No one angel performs two missions; nor do two angels perform the same mission.' Therefore, when two or more angels appear together they must have separate and different tasks to perform. This explains why no less than three angels visited Abraham (Genesis 18:1 ff). The midrash tells us they were Michael, Gabriel and Raphael. Raphael came to heal Abraham, who had just fulfilled God's command to circumcise himself. Michael bore the news that Sarah was to have a son. And Gabriel's purpose was to overthrow Sodom and Gomorrah and the other 'cities of the plain' (*Baba Mezia* 86b). The land of Israel being the most sacred of all countries in the world has special angels of its own, who do not venture beyond its borders. This explains the dream that Jacob had at Beth El. He saw a ladder with its top in the heavens, and 'the angels of God ascending and descending on it' (Genesis 28:12). One might have thought that the order of the verbs should be reversed. Surely angels come down from heaven first, and then go up again! But Scripture is really telling us that the angels who had accompanied Jacob so far were returning to heaven, and others were

---

*We have retained this name as being the one most generally known.
Modern critical scholars, however, believe that the correct translation should be 'Sea of Reeds', and that it refers to an expanse of water in Egypt near the Mediterranean shore.

descending, because Jacob was about to leave the Holy Land, and a different angelic retinue was required. (Commentary of Rashi.*)

Evil

The angels are, of course, by nature beneficent. They are the instruments of good. But one of the major problems that beset Jewish thinkers, as well as the proponents of any religion postulating the existence of a God who is both omnipotent and all-good, is the source of suffering and of evil. Judaism with its very strong emphasis on monotheism rejects utterly the existence of any power of evil that is equal in strength or authority to God. The Persian doctrine of two powers, one of light and one of darkness, threatened to encroach upon Jewish belief for a time, but was ousted, leaving only traces of its influence in some popular beliefs and customs. These, although not a significant area in what one might term 'mainstream' or 'normative' Judaism, do give rise to a wealth of legend and folklore, bordering on superstition on the one hand and mystical contemplation on the other.

The Bible already credits the one divine being as the source of all things. Isaiah says: 'I am the Lord, and there is none else. I form the light, and create darkness. I make peace, and create evil. I am the Lord that does all these things' (Isaiah 45:6f). How the spirits of evil actually came into the world was elaborated in later tradition. The concept of 'the fallen angels' appears in Pseudepigraphic literature, especially in the Book of Enoch (6–8; 12–16), where there is an extensive interpretation of a passage from Genesis (6:1–4). These puzzling verses describe the infatuation of 'the sons of God' with 'the daughters of men' and how as a result of their union 'mighty men' were born. That God disapproved of this state of affairs is deduced from the very next verse, which tells us that 'God saw that the wickedness of man was great in the earth and that every imagination of the thoughts of his heart was only evil continually.' To the author of the Book of Enoch the 'sons of God' were angels who lusted after women on earth. Their progeny were giants and

*The name by which Rabbi Solomon ben Isaac is commonly known. He is the most popular of all commentators to the Bible, and lived in Northern France, 1040–1105.

evil spirits. But the traditional Jewish commentators do not follow this interpretation. To them the 'sons of God' were human beings, judges and other men of authority, who acted presumptuously. For the origin of evil spirits they looked to another tradition which maintained that they were created by God at the very last moment, on the eve of the first Sabbath. He created spirits, but before he could clothe them in corporeal form the day of rest began, and so they remained without bodies. The fact that evil spirits, in popular imagination, do not throw shadows, is probably connected with this legend about their origin.

The world is populated by evil spirits, who occupy the same position in the realms of evil – 'the other side' – as angels do in heaven. They are presided over by two arch-demons, one female and one male: Lilith and Samael. Although popular etymology derives Lilith from *laylah* (night) her origin is probably to be sought in a Babylonian female demon named Lilitu. She was destined to be Adam's first wife, but she quarrelled with him and flew away. God sent three angels after her. They were called Snwy, Snsnwy, and Smnglf, and they found her in the Red Sea. They threatened her with the daily death of one hundred of her children if she did not return with them to Adam. But she stubbornly refused, and suffered the threatened punishment. (2 *Alphabet of Ben Sira* 23a–b, 33a–b.) Thenceforward, she attacked the newborn children of others. A baby boy is subject to her attacks for the first eight days of his life, and a baby girl for the first twenty days. In order to protect their children Jewish mothers in many parts of the world have resorted to magical amulets. These are of several kinds, and may bear the design of a hand, a menorah, a 'Star of David', a 'Seal of Solomon', or other geometrical patterns, with the accompaniment of suitable verses from Scripture, sometimes abbreviated to the first letter only of each word. Amulets were used to ward off sickness, to afford protection during a journey, and especially during childbirth. These latter often contain an image of Lilith, sometimes in chains, coupled with the names of the three angels who captured her. Occasionally, amulets bear a strange Hebrew alphabet, termed 'the Kabbalistic alphabet' or 'the alphabet of the angels', which has not yet been satisfactorily explained.

Lilith's progeny of evil spirits (*shedim*) is enormous. She could well afford to lose one hundred a day. In thirteenth-century kabbalistic literature she is known as the spouse of Samael, the prince of demons. Samael occurs in much earlier sources. In midrashic literature he appears as the guardian angel of Esau, and in the *Pirke de-Rabbi Eliezer* he rides the serpent who tempts Adam and Eve. He occupies an important place in the *Zohar* and in kabbalistic writings in general. One of the main ambitions of both himself and his supporting powers is to gain some hold on the Shekhinah (see p. 20). He is aided in this enterprise by the sins of man. But he can be placated or bribed. The sacrifices offered in the Temple were partly intended for the forces of evil to prevent them from interfering with the communion between man and the Shekhinah that took place at such times. The goat that was despatched to the demon Azazel on the Day of Atonement (Leviticus 16:10) was to the kabbalist an obvious offering of this type. The *Zohar* also states that the water used for washing the hands at meal times should be thrown away, as a bribe for 'the other side' in order to keep him at a proper distance.

The end of the sixth day of creation, that is, just before the beginning of the first Sabbath, was also the time when, according to rabbinic legend, the miraculous things were created, among them the mouth of Balaam's ass who spoke, the rainbow, the manna, Aaron's rod which turned into a serpent, the mouth of the well that sang (Numbers 21:16), and the shamir (see p. 151) that helped to construct the Temple, (*Mishnah Avot* 5:9). God also planned in the first days of the world that certain miracles should be performed for Israel: the Red Sea would part for the Israelites as they fled from Egypt; the sun would stand still for Joshua at Gibeon; the ravens would feed Elijah (*Genesis Rabbah* 5:4). This appreciation of divine foreknowledge was much approved by the great medieval Jewish philosopher, Maimonides, who saw in it an explanation of how the physical laws of nature could be interrupted by miraculous events. For him the miracles had already been 'written in' the laws that controlled the universe. They were not new phenomena, but old creations that had reached the time for them to be revealed.

When God created the world he was conscious of its whole destiny, and the destiny of the peoples who were to inhabit it. This is one of the most crucial of rabbinic insights into the nature of creation. God made a world which could endure. The aggadah tells us that he had created many worlds before this one, but none of them could survive because they had been ruled by the law of strict justice. Before he created the present world, therefore, he made repentance, so that human beings could temper divine justice with their own contrition. We have already seen (p. 20) that the Torah also existed before the creation. With these two elements, the divine law to guide mankind and repentance to bring him back from his erring ways, the world could escape annihilation.

Man

Man is at the centre of the world that God created. The first Biblical account places the creation of man at the very end of the sequence – the culmination of the divine activity. As the midrash points out it is only after the creation of man that God sees that his work is *very good*. He is 'made in the image of God' himself, and he is given dominion over all the other creatures on earth. The second account of creation places man even more firmly in the seat of power. Everything revolves round him. The whole story is about man – his potentiality, his vacillation and his failings.

The Biblical presentation of man's origins is not without its difficulties. In the first place, God's statement: 'Let us make man' (Genesis 1:26) implies that others beside God were involved in his creation, although modern scholars would say that here we have an example of the use of the 'royal we'. This phrase led the rabbis to propose that God was speaking to the angels, his retinue, and inviting them to join him in the creation of man. Many of them objected, pointing out man's future disobedience. But they were overruled by God, who compared man favourably with the angels, remarking that man had an evil inclination to overcome, whereas they were made without one. Hence the rabbinic dictum that 'where the penitent sinner stands, the perfectly righteous cannot stand'. This act of consultation on God's part, however, does display his humility and his willingness to seek the opinion of others, thus establishing a standard which human beings would do well to adopt for themselves. In the same way, God set an example to all judges by investigating himself the conduct of the builders of the Tower of Babel, since Scripture tells us 'The Lord came down to see the city and the tower . . .' (Genesis 11:5). It was only after verifying their wickedness with his own eyes that he punished them.

The idea that man is made in the divine image is also a difficult one for us to accept, especially since we have been brought up with the concept, derived from the Bible itself, that images of God are to be frowned upon. The context of the prohibition in the Ten Commandments about images is, of course, idolatry, the worshipping of physical figures or shapes which purport to represent some aspect of the divine or even an individual deity. The context of the creation story is quite different. Here we are dealing with a comparison between the power and position of man in relation to the physical world and that of God himself in relation to the universe. God gives man dominion over one, retaining for himself overriding control of all things. Man is therefore a finite model of the divine. This is not an uncommon feature in ancient Near Eastern mythology. In the Egyptian *Teaching of Ari* we read that 'Man is the counterpart of God', while *The Maxims of Khety*, which derive from the Middle Kingdom, teach us that human beings are 'replicas of God, which issue from his limbs.'

This correspondence between the human and the divine finds expression in reverse form in the *Talmud*, where we come across descriptions of God conducting himself in a quasi-human way, which go beyond the normal use of physical terminology to describe the divine. In *Berakhot* 7a we are told that God actually wears *tefillin* (phylacteries) when he prays. But what does he say in his prayers? 'May it be my will that my compassion overcome my anger, and that it may prevail over my attributes [of justice and judgment], and that I may deal with my children according to the attribute of compassion, and that I may not act towards them according to the strict line of justice.' Rabbi Judah, in the name of Rav, tells us how God spends his twelve-hour day: 'In the first three God sits and occupies himself with the Torah; in the next three he sits and judges the whole world, and whenever he sees that the whole world is guilty he rises from his throne of justice, and sits on the throne of mercy; in the next three he sits and feeds the whole world from the horned buffalo to the eggs of the louse; in the last three he sits and sports with Leviathan, as it says "Leviathan whom you have made to sport with" [Psalm 114:26]' (*Avodah Zarah* 3b). These anthropomorphic descriptions of God are, of course, no more to be taken literally than the Biblical statement that man was created in God's image.

Mythological parallels can also be adduced for the idea in the second account of creation that man was made from 'the dust of the ground'. The *Epic of Gilgamesh* tells how Enkidu was created by the goddess Aru who 'pinched off clay' and formed it in the divine image (2:35 ff) Notice also how Elihu says to Job, 'I am related to God as you are. I also am formed out of clay' (Job 33:6). The Biblical story has the additional significance that man's earthy origin explains his name. He is called 'Adam' because he was taken from the ground (*adamah*). This became the Hebrew term for the whole human species, so that when Jews wish to refer to the individual, Adam, they call him *Adam ha-rishon* 'the first Adam'.

According to the aggadah, God took a sample of earth from each of the four corners of the globe in order to create man, so that in whatever part of the world he died the earth could not disown him and refuse to receive his body. It is clear that the first man had to be of a universal type, representing the whole of mankind, and the *Talmud* (*Sanhedrin* 38a–b) even goes into specific details: the torso was taken from the soil of Babylon; the head from Palestine, and the extremities of the body from all the other parts of the world; while the genitals came from the site of a town called Akra de-Agma, which was notorious for the lust of its inhabitants.

The Soul

The earth, however, provided only the physical form of Adam. The soul came from God himself. At the end of human life 'the dust returns to the dust as it was, and the spirit returns to God who gave it' (Ecclesiastes 12:7). The soul, or spirit, or breath, which was breathed into Adam by God, is that element which turns matter into a living entity. There are three Hebrew words which designate this element: *ruah*, which also means 'wind'; *neshamah*, which means more specifically 'breath'; and *nefesh* which can also designate 'life' and 'self'. God breathes into Adam 'the neshamah of life', and he then becomes 'a living nefesh' (Genesis 2:7). The same phrase 'living nefesh' is used of animals too, in Genesis 1:30; while the living creatures that died in the Flood are designated as 'all that have in their nostrils the breath of the spirit of life' (*nishmat ruah hayyim*), (Genesis 7:22).

The fact that more than one term existed for 'soul' facilitated the view among medieval Jewish philosophers and mystics that there were three aspects of the human soul, or even three different souls within man, the lowest being the nefesh, which he had in common with the animal world, and the highest being the neshamah, with which he communicated with the divine.

Since the soul comes directly from God and is, in fact, the divine element within man, it is logical to assume that it pre-existed the creation of the world, or that, at least, it was among the first of created things. If it is identified with 'the spirit of God that hovered over the waters' it clearly preceded creation. In any event, it is a recognised rabbinic view that the souls of all mankind existed at the very beginning of creation, and that they remain stored beneath the divine Throne of Glory.

According to another view, the souls are all painted on the curtain which hangs in front of, and conceals, the divine throne. When a child is conceived God selects a particular soul from this store, and, despite its protests at being forced to leave the divine realm, plants it in the new embryo. God's selection is a careful one because he knows the future destiny of every human being from the point of birth onwards, and he chooses the soul that is most appropriate. An angel accompanies the soul on its journey to the lower world, and while it is still in the womb it teaches it all the mysteries of the universe. But as the new baby is about to be born the angel taps it lightly on the mouth, and the child forgets all that it has learnt. It therefore bursts into tears. Its whole life thence forward is a continual journey of discovery to try to recapture the wisdom which it has lost. (Jellinek, *Beth ha-Midrash* I, 153–5.)

The Platonic overtones of this view are quite evident, and it is easy to see how medieval Jewish philosophers could elaborate it in order to explain the human aspiration for knowledge of the divine.

The soul comes unsullied from its divine source. Part of the traditional morning liturgy reads 'O my God, the soul which you have given me is pure; you created it, you formed it, you breathed it into me; you preserve it in me; and you will take it from me, but will return it to me in the time to come' (Singer p. 6). It therefore exists uneasily in the world of matter. It yearns to return to its real home. The kabbalists maintained that the soul (or the highest aspect of it) does in fact visit its celestial abode at night while man is asleep, and is restored to him in the morning. This accounts for the visions of God that appear to the righteous at night-time. They are due to the communion that the soul is able to have with the divine. On the other hand, bereft of his total psychic faculties while he is asleep man is particularly vulnerable to evil spirits.

Regularly, however, man is able to have a foretaste of the life of the spirit even while he is bound to his terrestrial existence. The Sabbath is 'a foretaste of the world to come'. *Talmud Bezah* 16a tells us that man receives an additional soul on the eve of the Sabbath. And there are frequent references to the fact that two angels descend on the Sabbath to accompany the Jew to and from the synagogue. Both the additional soul and the angels depart as the Sabbath terminates. One of the purposes of the ritual of *Havdalah* which marks this termination is, symbolically, to prolong the sweetness of their presence by inhaling perfumes from a spice-box.

The After Life

The fate of the soul after death is the subject of much conjecture in Jewish tradition. Judaism is more concerned with fulfilling the commandments of God in this world than with any rewards in the world to come. And so there is no detailed systematic account agreed by all of the soul's progress after death. Furthermore there is an age-old exhortation not to speculate over much on 'what is above, what is beneath, what was before time, and what will be hereafter' (*Mishnah Hagigah* 2:1). Nevertheless, this advice did not prevent many and varied views of the after-life emerging. They all agree that the soul emanating from God himself must be immortal. But what happens to it once it leaves the body? The Bible speaks only of a shadowy world called *Sheol*, which is derived from a verbal root meaning 'ask'. This undefined area seems to be a kind of Hades, where recognisable individuals are to be found after their death. Isaiah refers to it in his prophecy concerning the King of Babylon:

> Sheol below is all astir
> To meet you at your coming;
> The shades are aroused for you,
> All the chief ones of the earth;
> All the kings of the nations
> Are raised up from their thrones . . .
> Your pride has been brought down to Sheol . . .
> (Isaiah 14:9–11).

It is no doubt from Sheol that the dead Samuel was raised at Saul's request by the witch of Endor.

The clearest enunciation of the concept of reward and punishment in the after-life occurs in Daniel (12.2–3), the youngest book in the Hebrew canon: 'Many of them that sleep in the dust of the earth shall awake, some to everlasting life, and some to reproaches and everlasting abhorrence. And they that are wise shall shine as the brightness of the firmament; and they that turn many to righteousness as the stars for ever.'

In post-Biblical times, however, the emphasis on reward and punishment in the after-life became stronger. And the Jewish preoccupation with the subject grew more intense as the rabbis grappled with the eternal problem of theodicy: the suffering of the righteous, and the prosperity of the wicked. How could a just and loving God allow this state of affairs to prevail? One solution of the problem, very commonly adduced in Jewish tradition, is that the righteous suffer in this world for the few sins they commit and will reap a great reward in the world to come, while the wicked are rewarded in this world for the few good deeds they have done and will suffer grievously in the world to come. Another solution, which the kabbalists favoured in particular, was to interpret events in terms of the soul's previous life. That a soul could transmigrate from one body to another was accepted by most Jewish mystics, and an individual's undeserved suffering could be laid at the door of the soul's previous habitation.

The custom in some Jewish communities of 'the beating at the grave' is connected with the expiation of sins in this world in order to avoid suffering in the next. As the coffin is taken to the grave it is lowered to the ground at regular intervals, this being a symbolic 'punishment' of the body. The soul is thought to hover near the body for some days after the burial, some authorities say for a much longer period – for almost a year – until a memorial stone is erected over the grave. Once this act of commemoration has been accomplished the soul can depart, but if the deceased's family fail to fulfil this obligation they condemn the soul to a terrestrial wandering existence.

The supreme reward of the righteous in paradise is 'to sit enthroned with crowns on their heads and enjoy the radiance of the Shekhinah' (*Berakhot* 17a). This is interpreted by some to mean that the righteous study Torah with God himself teaching them. The connection between the good life in this world and bliss in the hereafter is pithily summarised by a certain Rabbi Jacob: 'Better is one hour of repentance and good deeds in this world than the whole life of the world to come; and better is one hour of blissfulness of spirit in the world to come than the whole life of this world' (*Avot* 4:22). A more materialistic picture of the reward in store for the righteous is the great banquet which God has prepared for them, in which they will eat the delicious flesh of the sea-monster Leviathan.

The fate of the wicked in Gehinnom (hell) is not elaborated in the gory detail that we find in Christianity. This may be due not only to the reluctance of the rabbis to speculate over much on the after-life but also to the absence of a pictorial tradition. The sufferings of the wicked are real but according to most accounts not permanent. Gehinnom is a land of purgatory, and once they have paid for their iniquities the wicked can escape into a happier world. In any event, the torments of Gehinnom cease on the Sabbath, when even the wicked can enjoy God's peace.

It is a principle of traditional Judaism that the dead will experience physical resurrection at the end of days, and that this resurrection will take place in the Holy Land. One of the reasons why orthodox Jews will not permit cremation of the dead is the belief that resurrection will commence at one of the lower vertebrae of the spine, and that if therefore this vertebra is missing resurrection will be forestalled. The fact of resurrection in the Holy Land was taken literally enough to cause the rabbis some consternation about the underground journey that the dead who are buried outside the land will have to travel — a painful and troublesome experience. The midrash tells us that it was the thought of this journey that prompted Joseph to make his descendants swear that they would take his bones from Egypt with them when they eventually set out for the Promised Land. And still today pious Jews in the Diaspora keep by them a small bag of earth from the Holy Land which is to be put in their coffin, so that when the time comes they may be resurrected on the spot, on the soil of Israel, and avoid the long and tedious journey.

Clearly, some kind of judgment has to take place before the fates of the righteous and the wicked can be decided. Jewish tradition is vague concerning the order of events after death. The common phrase, 'the world to come', signifies both the immortal life of the spirit after death, the resurrection of the body, and the coming of the Messiah, or any one or more of these. But opinions vary concerning the relative positions of these phenomena in the chronological scheme of the last days. Somewhere within this sequence is the act of divine judgment.

Accounts of the divine judgment are many, and involve the full panoply of the court: angels for the prosecution, angels for the defence (these often being identified respectively with a man's evil and good deeds), clerks of the court, heralds, and God himself on the judgment-seat. The Jewish tendency to avoid an absolute dichotomy of body and soul is well illustrated in a parable related in the *Talmud* (*Sanhedrin* 91a). 'A certain Antigonus said to Rabbi Judah the Prince: Both body and soul could exempt themselves from punishment. The body could plead: "It was the soul that sinned. Since she left me I have lain here in the grave silent as a stone." And the soul could plead: "It was the body that sinned. Since I left it I have been flying in the air like a bird." Rabbi [Judah] said to him: Let me illustrate this with a parable. A king once had an orchard of beautiful fig-trees, and he appointed two men to guard it. One was lame and the other blind. The lame one said to the blind one: "I can see some beautiful figs in this orchard. Let me climb on your back, and I can pick them and then we can eat them." After a few days the owner came and said: "Where are my lovely figs?" The lame man said: "Can I walk about on these feet to get them?" The blind man said: "Have I got eyes to see them?"'

'What did the king do? He put the lame man on the blind man's back and judged them both together. Likewise the Holy One, blessed be He, will take the soul and put it back in the body and judge them both together.'

The final judgment is but the culmination of a series of annual judgments. And it is these latter which have indelibly imprinted themselves on the Jewish mind. The *Yamim Nora'im* (Days of Awe) which usher in the New Year set the scene for this divine assessment of human deeds. The theme is expressed in the image of a God who keeps a book of accounts of our actions. On the first day of the New Year he opens his book and begins to inscribe therein the names of those who are to survive throughout the coming year. Everything depends on the individual's past deeds, on his willingness to confess his sins and his determination not to repeat them. The opportunity to repent extends until the end of the tenth day, the Day of Atonement, when Jews fast as a token of contrition. The custom of visiting the graves of the deceased just before the Days of Awe is connected with the idea that the dead can intercede in heaven on behalf of the living, and goes back to the old belief that the patriarchs had stored up too much merit for themselves alone and could use the surplus for the benefit of others.

The desire to be inscribed in the Book of Life for the ensuing year is the overriding motive, whether conscious or unconscious, which impels Jews to visit their synagogues on the Days of Awe in far greater numbers than at any other time of the year. And the traditional New Year greeting expresses this desire for others: *Le-shanah tovah tikatevu ve-tihatemu* (May you be inscribed and sealed for a good year), usually abbreviated to *Le-shanah tovah* (For a good year).

BEFORE
THE
PATRIARCHS

Eden

W E HAVE already seen that the Jewish view of resurrection and the after-life is nowhere dogmatically presented in detail, and there is indeed lack of general agreement on many aspects of the subject. But in most descriptions of ultimate human destiny the Garden of Eden plays a prominent role. Although in later rabbinic tradition Eden became completely spiritualised in that it was seen as the abode of souls, both before their entry into the corporeal world and after their return from it, the original Biblical description places it firmly in the physical world. Four rivers flow from it, two of which are positively identified as the Tigris and the Euphrates, and therefore there can be little doubt that the head of the Persian Gulf was thought to be the geographical location of Eden. Sumerian mythology placed Eden, 'the abode of the gods', in Dilmon, which has been identified with Bahrain.

Eden became in the imagination of later generations the setting for the Golden Age of mankind, just as the desert in the time of Jeremiah became symbolic for the Golden Age of the Hebraic faith. Adam was to live happily here simply tending the trees which were to provide him with food (meat being apparently forbidden to man at this stage), but there were two trees which were put 'out of bounds': the Tree of Life which conferred immortality, and the Tree of Knowledge of Good and Evil. This latter tree was one which conveyed knowledge in general, not simply a moral awareness, the phrase 'good and evil' signifying all things, just as, for example, the phrase 'heaven and earth' indicated the whole universe. Otherwise, it is difficult to explain why God should not wish man to know the difference between good and evil. It is more comprehensible, even if not in accord with modern attitudes, to see God as being jealous of his own divine knowledge of the world in general. It is when man has achieved this knowledge that God concedes that he 'has become like one of us' and ensures, by driving him from Eden, that he does not eat of the Tree of Life and become immortal.

In the midrash the Tree of Life and the Tree of Knowledge are connected. In the very centre of the garden stood the Tree of Life and around it and protecting it, as it were, was the Tree of Knowledge, which was of prodigious size. One would have to travel for five hundred years just to circumnavigate the trunk, let alone explore the whole area beneath its branches (*Genesis Rabbah* 15:6). Did the Tree of Life then somehow grow out of the Tree of Knowledge? Such, it appears, was the view of one commentator on Genesis, Rabbenu Bahya ben Asher (d. 1340) who wrote that both trees 'formed one tree at the bottom, and branched out into two when they reached a certain height'.

The Bible does not specify the type of fruit which grew on the Tree of Knowledge. The rabbis made a number of suggestions, but, strangely enough, not one of them mentioned the apple, although this is the fruit which most people connect with Paradise. They do speak of 'the apple of Paradise', but they mean thereby the citron, which figures so largely in the Jewish festival of *Sukkot* (Festival of Tabernacles). Other interpretations are the grape, because no doubt wine was thought in the ancient world to be the drink of the gods, and also to arouse sexual desire (and Adam had relations with Eve only after they had eaten the fruit of the Tree of Knowledge); the fig, because it was with fig-leaves that the first human pair hid their nakedness; and, most extraordinarily, wheat, which, in Paradise, grew as high as the cedars in Lebanon. This last identification is based on the similarity of the Hebrew words *hita* (wheat) and *het* (sin).

The snake is well known in ancient mythology as the most intelligent and 'subtle' of all creatures, but the original tempter in the Garden of Eden was not, of course, a snake. It was only after the Fall that the serpent was cursed by God and as a result had to move on its belly and eat the dust of the ground. Before that time it had legs like other animals and according to one rabbinic tradition was like a man in appearance, standing upright on two legs. Therefore, the many representations of the temptation which depict the serpent as a snake curled round the Tree of Knowledge are really based on a misunderstanding of the scriptural text.

That the serpent's motive was primarily one of jealousy, either of the special favour that God had shown to man and woman, or of God's own wisdom and power, is attested by many sources. And the manner in which he encompassed his baleful task demonstrates his insidious nature. He seized upon an error made in all innocence by Eve. The serpent wished to ensnare her and so he asked her whether it was true that God had forbidden them to eat the fruit of the trees in the garden. She wishing to demonstrate the divine benevolence said: 'Of course not. We can eat any fruit we like. The only thing is we must not eat of the tree in the middle of the garden, *or touch it*; otherwise we shall die.' God, of course, had said nothing about touching the tree. It was Adam who had told her that, just to make absolutely sure that she did not fall into sin. The serpent seized his opportunity, and pushed Eve against the tree, so persuading her that there was no basis for the prohibition. It was all a matter of divine jealousy, and if she ate the fruit she would be like God, and would incur no danger. (*Genesis Rabbah* 19.)

What a change came over Adam and Eve after they had eaten the forbidden fruit! They lost their pristine glory. When he was first created Adam was so radiantly handsome that the sole of his foot outshone the brightness of the sun, and he was able to see from one end of the earth to the other. He was also protected from all possible harm by a shell-like skin. After the Fall his radiance was dimmed, and his skin became soft and vulnerable, except for his toe and finger nails which remained in their earlier state to remind him of his past glory. And to this day, at the end of the Sabbath, which is an earthly foretaste of life in paradise, Jews look at their finger nails by the light of the Havdalah candle to recall for a moment the goodness which God bestowed upon the first man in Eden.

Although Jews do not believe that the fall of Adam involved the whole of mankind thereafter in original sin, the Jewish mystics nevertheless looked upon the 'first man' in Paradise as the ideal receptacle for divine knowledge and instruction. And to the kabbalist the pristine Adam can still be revealed, albeit in a symbolic form, because the whole divine world of the sefirot, commonly represented as a tree in shape, can also be seen as forming the body of *Adam Kadmon*, primeval man, every organ having a mystical significance.

Cain

Cain, Abel and Seth, the three children of Adam and Eve, formed the second generation in the history of mankind. There were ten generations altogether before the arrival on the scene of Abraham, the first human being to recognise the one and only God. And these generations were, apart from a few special individuals like Enoch and Noah, totally wicked and corrupt. This is not really to be wondered at because they were largely descended from Cain, who himself, according to legend, was not Adam's child at all, but sired by the serpent Samael, who all along had cast lustful eyes upon Eve.

It seems from the scriptural story that the conflict between Cain and Abel represented the struggle between the nomadic shepherds and the more settled crop-farmers, which resulted in this case in the victory of the former since it was Abel's sheep-sacrifice that was accepted in preference to Cain's offering of 'the fruit of the ground'. But Jewish commentators preferred to explain things differently. Cain may have brought his contribution insincerely, or eaten most of it himself and offered God only the remnants. Others say that they actually quarrelled about the nature of God himself. Still others that Cain fell in love with Abel's sister, (for the midrash tells us that when Cain and Abel were born they were each accompanied by a twin sister), and his advances were rejected.

Whatever the reason Cain achieved for himself the dubious reputation of being the world's first murderer. Furthermore, since the Hebrew text, if translated literally, reads 'Listen, your brother's bloods [in the plural] cry to me from the earth' (Genesis 4:10) we may assume that God here accused Cain of killing not only Abel but all Abel's potential descendants as well. God, however, did not wreak vengeance upon Cain immediately; firstly, because Cain protested that he was ignorant as to the outcome of his actions since no one had ever seen death before, and he was not to know that a blow with a heavy stone would kill; and, secondly, because Cain was remorseful, exclaiming 'My sin is too great to bear' (Genesis 4:13). One beautiful interpretation of this verse makes of Cain a very pitiful figure appealing to God with the words 'Is my sin too great [for you] to bear?' And so God gave Cain 'a sign' to protect him. What this sign actually was the Bible does not specify. Some say that it was a letter of the divine name, since the Hebrew word for 'sign' (*ot*) also means 'letter'; others that he marked him with the sign of leprosy; still others, most charmingly, that God gave him a dog for his protection.

Another view is that a horn grew out of his forehead, and that it was this that finally led to Cain's downfall. He survived until the seventh generation and then he was killed by Lamech. It happened like this. Lamech liked to hunt, but he was blind, and he relied on his son to search out his quarry for him. One day the son saw a horned creature and pointed his father in that direction, telling him at exactly the right moment to shoot with his bow and arrow. The arrow found its target. They approached the body and when Lamech touched the horn on the forehead he realised at once that this was 'the sign', and that he had killed Cain. (*Tanhuma Bereshit* II.)

The genealogical lists of the descendants of Cain and Seth have puzzled generations of Bible readers, particularly because of the longevity that is assigned to them. It should be remembered, however, that these antediluvian heroes were thought to be something more than human, since they were so close to the beginning of the world, and that from that Golden Age man has experienced a steady physical decline. The length of their lives is therefore symbolic of their supra-human characters. The same can be said of parallel lists in other Near Eastern cultures: the lists of kings among the Sumerians for example, whose life-spans were longer than those of their Biblical counterparts. Another obvious, but often overlooked point is that because of their longevity the 'generations' were for much of their lives contemporaneous. The ten generations from Adam to Noah covered no more than 1656 years, although individuals each lived for eight or nine hundred years or more. Noah did not die until Abraham was sixty! This chronology, however, was taken seriously enough by the rabbis for them to use it as a basis for their dating system. The Jewish calendar counts its years from the creation of the world. Hence, the year 1979 AD (CE) approximates to the Jewish year 5739 AM (*anno mundi*).

Among these long-lived patriarchs Enoch is something of an exception. He is already singled out for special comment in the Bible. 'Enoch walked with God, and was not; for God took him'

(Genesis 5:24), and the fact of the matter is that he died young. He lived to be only 365. The very brief reference in the Bible to the special case of Enoch clearly conceals a more detailed legend about him which is now lost. But it gave rise in turn to subsequent stories concerning his great wisdom and sanctity, and the close relationship he enjoyed with God. In the pseudepigraphic writings, the *Ethiopian Book of Enoch*, the *Slavonic Book of Enoch*, the *Book of Jubilees*, as well as in the literature of the Dead Sea sect, Enoch occupies a very high place. He was instructed by the angels, indeed by God himself, in the mysteries of the universe, and he did not die as other mortal men, but, very like Elijah in later times, was 'taken up' to God in heaven. These stories about Enoch, however, seemed to circulate only in esoteric circles or among Jewish sectarians, because there is no reference whatsoever to him in either the Babylonian or the Palestinian Talmud. His adoption by the Church as a Christological figure no doubt contributed to his being comparatively ignored in earlier Jewish rabbinic literature. He does, however, reappear in kabbalah where he is identified with the angel Metatron.

The Flood

The story of Noah and the Flood is one of the most familiar episodes in the whole Biblical narrative. It has been reworked many times in music, drama and art, and the scene of the animals entering the ark two by two has impressed itself on the imagination of countless generations of children.

The legend itself is older than its actual narration in Genesis. It probably arose from a real and disastrous inundation of the Mesopotamian basin, which was then recounted orally in mythological form from one age to the next. The closest and most detailed parallel to the Biblical story is the flood episode in the *Epic of Gilgamesh*. There too the hero, Utnapishtim, is warned of the impending disaster, and advised to make a boat. The description of the flood itself is similar, and the hero uses birds, including a dove and a raven, to ascertain whether the flood waters are decreasing. But the dissimilarities are no less striking, especially those that illustrate the differences in their theological and moral backgrounds. The reason given in the Bible for the divine displeasure is man's moral corruption, whereas in the Gilgamesh epic the gods are enraged because the noise that humanity made was so loud that they could not sleep: 'the world bellowed like a wild bull, and the great god was aroused by the clamour ... the uproar of mankind is intolerable, and sleep is no longer possible .... So the gods in their hearts were moved to let loose the deluge.' Noah, to celebrate his rescue, offered a sacrifice to God 'and the Lord smelled the sweet savour', whereas the Sumerian gods in addition 'gathered like flies over the sacrifice'.*

The sins which were being committed on earth were of such a nature that God felt he had no option but to destroy that whole generation. The Bible describes the world as being corrupt and full of violence. The rabbis interpreted this to mean that the people were sexually perverse and licentious, and that they were rapacious towards one another. Even when opportunities were given to them to repent they were obdurate and would not change their ways.

Only Noah and his family were to survive and lay the foundation for a new world. It was obvious from the very moment of Noah's birth that he was destined for great things. A resplendent light was emitted from his whole body, and his father Lamech went to the child's grandfather Methuselah to ascertain the significance of this remarkable sight. Methuselah in turn repaired to Enoch who knew all the mysteries of the universe. Enoch consulted the wonderful *Book of Raziel* that had originally been given to Adam, and there he read of the part that Noah was to play in the salvation of the human race. Noah's future role could also have been predicted from the fact that he was born circumcised, a feature that was common only to Adam, Seth and Melchizedek, of those born before Abraham.

The statement in the Bible about Noah's virtues is, however, somewhat ambiguous. It says that 'he was righteous in his generation' (Genesis 6:9). This may mean that even in so corrupt an age as his he was righteous, and he would have been even more righteous had he lived in a better age. Or it could mean that compared with the rest of humanity at that time he was righteous, but had he lived in a more virtuous age he would not have been so outstanding. (*Genesis Rabbah* 30:10.)

In contrast to later Christian stories about Noah's wife, particu-

---

The Epic of Gilgamesh translated by N. Sandars, Penguin, 1970, pp. 105-9.

larly in the English medieval 'mystery' plays, she is portrayed in Jewish legend as invariably helpful and supportive of her husband. This is not to be wondered at because she was a daughter of the virtuous Enoch, named Na'amah. His three sons, Shem, Ham and Japhet, also co-operated. It was Noah himself who had the occasional doubt, and he was not really convinced of the immediacy of the danger until the flood water had reached his knees.

By this time all the occupants were safely installed in the ark. The animals had come to Noah of their own accord, because it would have been impossible for him to have collected them all together. Only the fish of course had no need to come. Noah had a particular problem with the fabulous huge monster, the re'em. The ark was not big enough to accommodate it, so it had to be towed behind (*Genesis Rabbah* 31). Another survivor was the giant Og, King of Bashan. He rode out the emergency, sitting on the roof (*Pirke de-Rabbi Eliezer* 23).

The task of feeding the animals during the year that the Flood lasted was a monumental one. The particular diet of each creature had to be ascertained and provided for, and, furthermore, their individual feeding-times had to be strictly adhered to. It is said that Noah was assaulted by the lion simply because he was late with its food, and that he limped ever after as a result. The animals of prey had to be kept at a distance from their natural quarries. Noah's family had, in addition, to attend to the problem of cleaning the animals' quarters. According to a tradition cited by Rashi the lowest of the three stories of which the ark was composed was reserved for waste matter. These problems were made a little easier in that there was no procreation, either human or animal, in the ark, for it was not appropriate that creatures should indulge themselves in such pleasures while the rest of the world was plunged in tragedy.

When the rains had ceased, and the waters began to subside, Noah despatched birds to find out whether the tops of the trees had begun to appear. He first sent the raven, but not without some objections on the raven's part. He was an unclean animal and therefore there was only a single pair of them in the ark. 'Why not send a clean animal?' the raven protested. 'There are seven each of them. If I die the whole raven species will disappear.' But Noah insisted, and in retaliation the raven would not come back. He found some carrion and remained on dry land gorging himself

(*Sanhedrin* 108a–b). The second time, therefore, Noah did choose a clean bird. The dove was more faithful, and eventually returned with an olive-branch in her beak, thus indicating that the time would soon arrive for them all to disembark. Actually the 'sign' was not totally reliable because the dove had taken the twig from the Mount of Olives and the Holy Land had escaped the Flood altogether!

Noah and his family became the ancestors of a new breed of men, all the other descendants of Adam having been destroyed. In order that future generations should not through their folly endanger the continuity of the human race God gave Noah seven fundamental laws which were thenceforward incumbent upon the whole of mankind. They are called 'the laws of the sons of Noah.' The rabbis held that these precepts were intended by God to apply to all peoples, even if they refused to accept all the 613 commandments of the Torah. The seven are as follows: 'You shall not worship idols; you shall not blaspheme; you shall not murder; you shall not commit incest; you shall not rob; you shall establish courts of law; you shall not eat the flesh of a living animal' (*Sanhedrin* 56a). This last was significant because it was only after the Flood that man was permitted to eat flesh, and certain provisos had to be instituted, including the prohibition of eating the blood of an animal.

Noah is credited in Jewish legend with being an inventor of farming implements, since he had the daunting task of recultivating the soil. Some of his new discoveries, however, had unfortunate consequences; for example, the institution of viticulture which resulted in Noah's becoming drunk and exposing himself to his family.

During their stay in the ark Noah's family not unnaturally suffered considerable privation and their cramped conditions and proximity to the animals made them ill, causing diseases of which they had no previous experience. To remedy this situation Shem was taken by one of the angels to paradise in the East where he was given a wonderful Book of Medicines. This book was the origin of all later medical works. Indeed, all the scientific and philosophic writings of the Greeks and other nations were derived from the knowledge that was granted to Shem. (Jellinek, *Beth ha-Midrash* III, 155.)

Shem's descendants were allotted the Holy Land as their inheritance, this being at the centre of the world. Ham was the ancestor of all the inhabitants of Africa, and among Japhet's descendants were the Greeks. Seventy nations in all comprised the total population of the world, a figure which was deduced from the list in Genesis 10. (*Midrash ha-Gadol* I, 196.)

The Tower of Babel

At first they all spoke the same language and understood one another perfectly, but they were deprived of this boon because they rebelled against God. According to most rabbinic traditions the leader of this rebellion was Nimrod. He is described in the Bible as a great hunter, but he was more than that. He was the most powerful ruler that the world had seen up to that date. He gained his prowess from the magical clothes that he wore. They were the very garments that God had given to Adam and Eve when they left the Garden of Eden. Made out of the skin of Leviathan, they rendered the wearer invisible and victorious over all his enemies. They had come down by inheritance to Noah, but Ham had stolen them in the ark, and had given them to his son, Cush, who had handed them on to *his* son, Nimrod. (*Sefer ha-Yashar, Noah* 17a.)

Nimrod prevailed upon all the other peoples to build a great tower as a central focus to prevent their being scattered over the face of the earth. But his main intention was to make war upon God in heaven. They even erected a statue at the top of the tower with a sword in its hand, threatening heaven. The tower took more than forty years to build, and a whole year was needed to climb to the summit. One of the most heinous sins of this generation was their attachment to material things. If a man or woman fell from the tower during its construction they paid no heed, but if a brick fell they made sure that it was retrieved (*Pirke de-Rabbi Eliezer* 24). On the other hand, their one redeeming feature was that they lived in harmony with one another. That was the reason why God did not utterly destroy them as he did the generation of the Flood. In the end, he frustrated their design by confusing their tongues. They suddenly found themselves speaking different languages, and they could no longer understand one another. As the midrash puts it: A said to B, 'Pass me my axe'. B thereupon handed him a hammer. They came to blows, and the tower remained unfinished and eventually deserted.

ABRAHAM

THERE WERE a few among Nimrod's subjects who refused to participate in the building of his tower. The most famous of these was Abraham, who had in his infancy already perceived that there was but one God, Master of the universe and of the whole of mankind.

With Abraham the Bible narrative moves from the history of man to an account of the origins of a single people, the Hebrew nation, and of that nation's growing commitment to the service of God. As the scene of the action becomes more confined, concentrating on specific geographical areas and on particular families, so we move from pre-history to events which receive progressively firmer substantiation from sources outside the Bible itself. Individual names, places, customs and laws have their parallels in the historical documents of other ancient Near Eastern peoples.

Jewish legend, however is not concerned with historicity. Its main purpose is to extol the virtues of the patriarchs, by dwelling lovingly on every detail of their recorded exploits, and to portray them as models of devotion, courage, and piety. Abraham, 'the friend of God', was a figure particularly loved and admired by the rabbis. It was his faith and utter subservience to God which formed the basis of the Jewish people as 'a holy nation'. Only Moses was able to equal Abraham in pre-eminence in the Jewish tradition.

The stories surrounding the infancy of Abraham are, in fact, obviously influenced by those in the Bible that concern Moses. Nimrod is told by his magicians and sorcerers that a male child is to be born who will grow up to be his mortal enemy. He therefore issues an edict that all pregnant women should be brought to a special place when their time is nigh, and that every baby boy born there should be killed. In order to escape the possibility of losing her child Abraham's mother conceals her pregnancy from her husband

Terah, who is a faithful follower of Nimrod, and goes to a cave in a deserted spot to await the birth of her son. She is helped by the angel Gabriel. When Abraham is born he, like Noah, irradiates a resplendent light, and his mother in stupefaction leaves him. Gabriel sees to it that the child does not starve by causing milk to flow from the baby's little finger.

While still in infancy Abraham recognised the true God. At first he fell to worshipping the stars, but when the moon rose and outshone the stars, this became the object of his devotions. At dawn he switched his allegiance to the rising sun, and when this was obscured by cloud, he realised that there was an unseen God who controlled all these natural forces, none of which was worthy of his undivided loyalty. (*Genesis Rabbah* 38.)

Abraham therefore resolved to persuade others of his new faith, and to crush the idolatry that was rampant in Nimrod's domains. He was reunited with his mother and father, who earned his living at Nimrod's court by making idols. One day when his father was away Abraham smashed all the idols in his workshop, leaving just one in whose hand he placed a hammer. When Terah returned Abraham accused this one idol of destroying all the others. Terah protested that that was impossible. 'How then,' retorted his son, 'can you worship an image that has no power?'

Nimrod decided that such a threat to his authority as Abraham posed had to be got rid of. He therefore made a fiery furnace for Abraham. This was one of the trials which the patriarch had to undergo to prove his faith. The story is clearly based on the similar story narrated in the Book of Daniel. And like the three heroes in that story Abraham survives with the aid of one of the angelic host. Nimrod and his retinue were amazed to see Abraham in the fire, apparently taking his ease in what seemed to be a reconstruction of the Garden of Eden (Jellinek, *Beth ha-Midrash* I, 33).

Abraham, at God's behest, left Nimrod's kingdom to journey to an unknown destination. The fact that he agreed to undertake such a journey was evidence of his utter trust in God. He took with him his wife Sarah, who was the daughter of his older brother, Haran, and 'the souls that they had made' (Genesis 12:5). This phrase refers to those who had become converted to the new faith. Abraham converted the men, and Sarah the women. Still today a convert to Judaism is named 'son' or 'daughter' of 'Abraham, our father'.

Jonah being spewed out by the fish. A drawing in micrography.
Pentateuch, *megillot*, and Job. Franco-German, thirteenth to fourteenth
centuries.
British Library, London. MS Add. 21160, fol. 292r.

Leviathan and the wild-ox. Folk-art. Zawichost, Poland. Nineteenth century.

R. Lilientowa, 'Swięta żydowskie w przeszlości i terazniejszości', Cracow, 1908, Tab. 2.

Top Fragments of ivory figures, probably Cherubim, from the Assyrian palace at Nimrud. It is thought that they were made in Phoenicia and that they were later taken as booty to Nimrud. Eighth century BCE.
British Museum, London.

Above The animals entering the Ark. Floor mosaic from the synagogue at Gerasa, fifth century CE.
Department of Antiquities, Amman.

Amulet for the protection of a new-born child. Baghdad, sixteenth to
seventeenth centuries.
Collection of Isaac Einhorn, Tel Aviv.

Top Amulet for pregnant women, showing in each compartment
representations of the three angels who captured Lilith.
Sefer Raziel: Amsterdam, 1701.

Above The so-called 'alphabet of the angels'.
Sefer Raziel: Amsterdam, 1701.

Top Dish, silver gilt, showing the binding of Isaac, and signs of the zodiac. *Vienna (?), 1835. Jewish Museum, London.*

Above Abraham destroying the idols. *Haggadah.* German, 1740. *British Library, London MS Add. 18724, fol. 7r.*

Abraham in Nimrod's fiery furnace, and the Sacrifice of Ishmael, showing
Muslim adaptations from Jewish themes. *Zubdat al-Tawārīkh* by Luqmān-
i-Ashūrī, Turkey, *c.* 1583.
Chester Beatty Library, Dublin, MS 414, fol. 68v.

Scenes from the life of Jacob. Shalom of Safed (Shalom Moskovitz).
Gouache on paper, 1959.
Sir Isaac and Lady Wolfson Museum in Hechal Shlomo, Jerusalem.

56

Ark Curtain, Italy, 1681, showing panorama of Jerusalem. Purple silk,
embroidered with silk and metallic thread by Simha, wife of Menahem Levi
Meshullam.
Jewish Museum, New York.

Potiphar's wife attempting to seduce Joseph. Pewter dish. Eastern Europe, *c.* 1815.
Státní Židovské Muzeum, Prague.

Challah cloth for Sabbath-eve, showing two loaves to represent the double portion of manna that fell in the wilderness on Friday. German, nineteenth century.
Hebrew Union College Skirball Museum, Los Angeles, California.

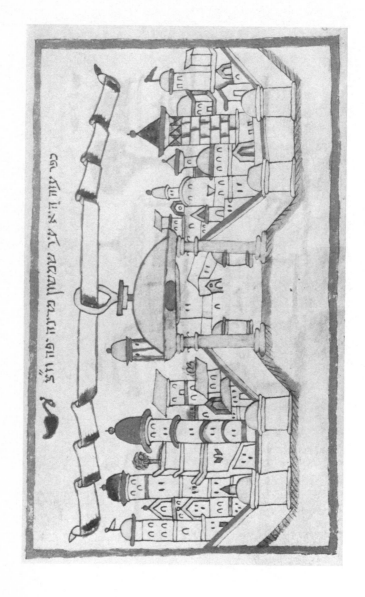

The city of Gaza, scene of Samson's exploits. Casale, Pilgrim MS. Casale
Monferrato, Italy, 1568.
The Brotherton Library, University of Leeds MS Roth 220 fol. 9v.

The ten plagues. Woodcut by Jakob Steinhardt. *Haggadah*, Berlin, 1923.
Ansbacher Collection, Jerusalem.

The recital of the Exodus from Egypt, with the Seder at the foot.
Darmstadt *Haggadah*. German, fifteenth century.
Hessische Landes- und Hochschulbibliothek, Darmstadt Cod. Or. 8, fol. 37v.

The Israelites crossing the Red Sea, illustrating the midrash that each tribe had a path of its own. Rylands *Haggadah*. Spain fourteenth century. *John Rylands University Library, Manchester, MS 6, fol. 19r.*

Moses bringing the Ten Commandments down from Mount Sinai.
Regensburg Pentateuch, *c.* 1300.
Israel Museum, Jerusalem. MS 180/52, fol. 154v.

Another trial which Abraham had to face was the famine in Canaan. In order to escape it he went down to Egypt, and it was as he crossed into Egypt that he realised for the first time how beautiful his wife was. In the words of the Bible, Abraham said to Sarah 'Now I know you are a beautiful woman' (Genesis 12:11). How is it that he had not discovered this fact previously? The answer is that Abraham lived a very chaste life and had not even looked at his wife before. But as they were crossing a river to enter Egypt his downward gaze saw her reflection in the water, and only then did he appreciate her beauty (Rashi; *Sifte Hakhamim*). His ruse in passing off Sarah as his sister worried many later commentators. We now know that the Hurrians, among whom Abraham had lived in Mesopotamia, had a legal custom by which husbands 'adopted' their wives as their sisters. This intitution seems to have become obscure by the time the Biblical account was written; hence the details of the story. The midrash points out that Abraham and Sarah's sojourn in Egypt had happy results. Not only did Pharaoh give Abraham flocks and herds, but he assigned to Sarah the land of Goshen, later to be occupied by her descendants, and he also gave her his own daughter, the princess Hagar, to be her servant-girl (*Pirke de-Rabbi Eliezer* 26).

It was soon after his return to Canaan that Abraham had a vision at night of the future history of his descendants. God informed him of the four hundred years of slavery that the Hebrews were to suffer in Egypt; and in the Covenant between the Pieces (Genesis 15) God showed him how the Jews would suffer under many foreign rulers but would eventually emerge triumphant. All this was partly to reassure Abraham, because up to that time he had not been blessed with the gift of children.

The divine command that Abraham should circumcise both himself and his male descendants is linked in the Bible both with a promise of future greatness, and also with a change of name. This is the first example of such a change. He was to be henceforth called Abraham instead of Abram, and Sarai was to be renamed Sarah. The rabbis were not slow to point out that to both names God added the letter H, the letter that occurs twice in the ineffable name of God himself, YHVH. And it is not without significance that it was only after the circumcision and the change of name that Abraham and Sarah together had their child Isaac. Circumcision has, of course, become a most important ritual in Jewish belief and practice. Even the least observant Jew will not lightly dispense with it. Name-changing too has its place in Jewish custom. A child who is very ill will often be given a different or additional name, the most common being Hayyim (for a boy) or Hayyah (for a girl), both of them meaning 'life'.

The birth of Isaac was foretold to Abraham, and to an incredulous Sarah, by three angels. Two of these went on to Sodom. The destruction of Sodom and the other cities of the plain was caused not only by the sexual perversity of their inhabitants but also by their pitiless voracity. They were a byword for their hatred of strangers. They had strict orders from their superiors not to offer hospitality to passers-by. Anyone found offering a crumb to travellers, however needy and destitute they might be, was put to death. They also had a perverse scale of values. The poorer you were the less reward you received for your work. When Abraham's servant, Eliezer, visited Lot in Sodom, he was stoned, and blood poured from a wound in his forehead. He went to the local judge to lodge a complaint, and the judge told him that he would have to pay for the privilege of having his blood let (*Sefer ha-Yashar, Va-yera*).

Nevertheless, Abraham, who was the acme of generosity, hospitality and compassion, prayed to God to have mercy on the towns because of the righteous people who might live there. There is a Jewish tradition that every generation needs at least thirty-six righteous men. Otherwise it cannot survive. Abraham went even further and pleaded for the cities provided there were ten righteous men living there. Abraham did not bother to proceed to a lower figure because he knew from the example of the Flood that it would have been of no use (*Genesis Rabbah* 49).

At the destruction of Sodom Lot's wife was punished for looking back. The similarity with the Orpheus and Eurydice story is obvious, and it is a motif which is common in legends. The rabbis presumed that she looked back because she was concerned about the fate of her two married daughters who had been left behind, and she saw the Shekhinah at work destroying the cities (*Pirke de-Rabbi Eliezer* 25). The pillar of salt was still apparently identified in Talmudic times, since it is stated in *Berakhot* (54a–b) that one should say two blessings on seeing it, one praising God 'the true Judge' which is usually recited at a time of bereavement, and one praising God 'for remembering the righteous', i.e. for rescuing Lot.

The promise that the angels gave to Abraham was fulfilled when a son, Isaac, was born to Sarah. Any doubts that their contemporaries might have had concerning Isaac's parentage, in view of the great age of Abraham and Sarah, were quickly dispelled. First of all, Isaac looked exactly like his father, and secondly Sarah had so much milk in her breasts that she was able to nurse all the babies in the vicinity. These babies gained great advantage from the matriarchal nourishment. They became the ancestors of all the sincere proselytes to Judaism, and of all the righteous among the Gentile nations (*Genesis Rabbah* 53).

The relationship of Ishmael and Isaac to their father Abraham, on the one hand, and to their spiritual descendants, on the other, has been the subject of profound enquiry and great controversy. The Jews trace their ancestry to Abraham through Isaac, while the Muslims claim their Abrahamic inheritance through Ishmael. This critical difference of opinion is reflected in the legends of the two faiths concerning Abraham's two sons. An obvious overlapping of tradition is seen in a story in which Abraham in disguise visits Ishmael's home. As a result of his visit Ishmael divorces his first wife and marries a second time. The names of his two wives are Aisha and Fatima, the same as the names of Mohammed's wife and daughter (*Pirke de-Rabbi Eliezer* 30).

Muslims claim that they are the true heirs of Abraham because Ishmael was his first-born, while the Jews point out that Ishmael's mother was a servant-girl, whereas only Isaac shared the blood of both Abraham and Sarah. This competition is reflected in a midrash (*Sanhedrin* 89b) which tells of an argument between the two sons. Ishmael boasts that he is the more worthy because he was thirteen years of age when he was circumcised and had to display considerable courage, while Isaac was but a baby, eight days old, and knew nothing at all about it. Isaac retorts by saying that if he were required to sacrifice his whole life in the service of God he would willingly do so.

The Binding of Isaac

Such a sacrifice was, of course, required of him; although Muslims reinterpret the whole episode, believing that it was Ishmael and not Isaac who accompanied Abraham on that fateful journey to the mountain to be sacrificed. For the Jews, of course, there can be no doubt as Genesis 22 specifically mentions Isaac. The pathos and drama of this story as well as the simple and direct method of its telling make it one of the great seminal episodes in Western cultural history. The reverberations of the event continue to echo down the ages. The absolutely trusting nature of Abraham, who was willing to offer up the son whom he had desired so passionately for so many years, and the noble and courageous resignation of Isaac, who was no child (tradition states that he was thirty-seven) and knew exactly what was planned, have impressed themselves on the Jewish mind as the supreme example of perfect faith. This passage is read in the synagogue on New Year's Day, the beginning of the Season of Penitence, to remind the worshippers of what true devotion to God might entail.

Yet − and this is an obvious but nevertheless necessary remark − Isaac was not sacrificed. However bitter and painful the test, it was sufficient that Abraham and Isaac showed themselves ready. The actual immolation was not required. That is why the episode in Jewish tradition is called the binding (*Akedah*) of Isaac, not the sacrifice of Isaac. By this name the Jews dissociate themselves from Christian interpretations, which see in Isaac's experience a prefigure-ment of the Christian story.

The theological problem of why God found it necessary to put Abraham through such an agonising experience is one that is still actively discussed. One of the main reasons proposed is that a public demonstration was required of faith in God in order to convince the unbelievers of divine sovereignty. At the same time, however, God is portrayed in the aggadah as being sympathetic to Abraham's position. His opening command 'Take your son, your only one, whom you love, Isaac' is seen as a carefully graded approach, meant to break the news in as gently a fashion as possible. 'Your son' could have meant Isaac or Ishmael: 'your only one' likewise, because Isaac was the 'only' son of Sarah, and Ishmael the 'only' son of Hagar; 'whom you love' did not make things clearer, because Abraham loved them both. It was only when the name 'Isaac' was pronounced that Abraham understood exactly what God demanded (*Sanhedrin* 89b).

The whole episode can also be seen not only as a demonstration of faith but as a rejection of human sacrifice. The substitution of the ram is an integral part of this view. But for the rabbis the ram was a special one. It had eternal as well as local significance. Its skin provided a mantle for Elijah, its gut the strings of David's harp, and its two horns the two trumpets: one to be sounded later at the great revelation of God at Mount Sinai, and the other to be blown at the end of time to announce the coming of the Messiah (*Pirke de-Rabbi Eliezer* 31). And the actual site of the altar which Abraham had constructed was the very same place where Abel and Noah had offered their sacrifices, and the very site of the Temple that was to be erected in years to come. This kind of interpretation, however far fetched in literal terms, serves to place the Akedah in a symbolic context. It is related in detail to all the other significant phenomena of Jewish religious experience, and illustrates the rabbinic dictum that there is no 'early or late' in the Torah, i.e. the chronology is not important. Everything is contemporaneous. Or, as a more modern observer might put it, 'every age is equidistant from eternity'.

Since in the scriptural account the death of Sarah follows soon after the narration of the binding of Isaac, it was natural for later tradition to connect the two events. According to one legendary account Satan told Sarah that Abraham had gone to sacrifice Isaac, and Sarah was so distraught that she went in search of them, going as far as Hebron. There she received news that her son was safe, and she was overcome with such great joy that she died (*Sefer ha-Yashar, Va-yera*). Another version states that Isaac had been slightly harmed by Abraham during the Akedah and that in order to be perfectly healed he was taken to paradise for three days. In the meantime Abraham returned home on his own. When Sarah saw that Isaac was not with him, she died of grief (*Midrash ha-Gadol* I, 360).

The place that Abraham selected for her burial was the Cave of Machpelah in Hebron, which has been a place of pilgrimage for Jews, Christians and Muslims for centuries. Abraham chose this particular site because it was the burial place of Adam, Eve and Seth, and he also knew that those buried there would be the first to be resurrected in the latter days. The Bible goes out of its way to stress the fact that Abraham actually purchased the site from Ephron, the Hittite, in the presence of witnesses, in order to counter any claim that the Hebrews had no right of possession.

The *Zohar* (I, 128a–b) contains the extraordinary legend that when Abraham came to bury Sarah in Machpelah, Adam and Eve were overcome by shame at their misdemeanour in the Garden of Eden and wanted to give up their places to the righteous Sarah. But Abraham prayed on their behalf, and restored them to their place of rest. Two other patriarchal couples are also buried here: Isaac and Rebecca, and Jacob and Leah. Hebron became a centre of the national kingdom, before the conquest of Jerusalem, because it was in Hebron that David was proclaimed king. Although in the early Middle Ages Jews had access to Hebron and Machpelah, the actual site of the cave was forbidden to Jews by the Sultan Baybars in 1267. It was only 700 years later, after the 1967 war, that Jews were once more able to worship there.

When Abraham himself died at the age of 175 he was buried in Machpelah by both his sons, Ishmael and Isaac (Genesis 25:9), thus showing in the view of the rabbis that there had been a reconciliation between Abraham and Ishmael.

For Jews Abraham is not only the first monotheist. He is the father of the Jewish people, the first of the patriarchs. There are even those who maintained that he observed all the 613 commandments of the Torah, even though he died long before the Torah was revealed to the Hebrew people at Mount Sinai. He is characterised in legend principally by his far-reaching hospitality, his firm faith, and his deep compassion for his fellow creatures. Moreoever it is with Abraham that God first makes the promise, repeated in successive generations, that he will give 'the land' to the Hebrews, Abraham's descendants. 'The land' is variously defined, its geographical borders being inconsistently described. But at its narrowest it is the land of Canaan (Genesis 12:7), while at its broadest it stretches from Egypt to the Euphrates (Genesis 15:18).

The *Talmud* (*Baba Batra* 91a–b) tells us that when Abraham died the heads of all the nations in the world went into mourning, saying: 'Alas for the world that has lost its leader! Alas for the ship that has lost her helmsman.' And the whole of Canaan mourned for twelve months.

JACOB

OF THE three patriarchs Isaac is the one who is the least clearly portrayed in Scripture, and consequently the rabbis and the Jewish people generally were not able to find in the Biblical text those particular details which lend themselves so easily to elaboration in folk-tale and legend. It is in connection with his father on the one hand, and his children on the other that he really comes into prominence. He is not so memorable as a personality in his own right.

Nevertheless, the rabbinic tradition insists that he is given equal respect and honour with Abraham and Jacob. The core of the Jewish liturgy is the *Amidah*, and this begins: 'O God, and God of our fathers, God of Abraham, God of Isaac, and God of Jacob.' Why is the name of God mentioned separately with each of the patriarchs? Would it not have been simpler to say 'God of Abraham, Isaac and Jacob'? One of the traditional answers to this question is that each of the patriarchs had a different perception of God, so that looked at subjectively, from the point of view of the individual, the 'God of Abraham' was different from the 'God of Isaac', who again differed from the 'God of Jacob'; although, of course, objectively there is only one God.

The institution of the three daily prayers, Morning, Afternoon and Evening, is also equally shared among the patriarchs. Abraham is credited with the Morning Prayer, Jacob with the Evening Prayer; and, as for Isaac, Rebecca encountered him for the first time 'musing in the field' (Genesis 24:63). Some say he was lamenting the death of his mother, Sarah. But others maintain that he was praying, and by doing so he instituted the regular Afternoon Prayer (*Genesis Rabbah* 60).

If Isaac is a somewhat shadowy figure, Jacob, his son, is a fully formed character already in the pages of Scripture, not to speak of the many legends that are connected with his name and his exploits.

No Biblical story is more subtle in all its ramifications than the story of Jacob, and the portrayal of him is especially appealing to us because, far more than his father, or grandfather, he is a recognisable human being. He has his faults and his virtues. At one moment he seems to be a weak, vacillating creature, a plaything of forces that are more powerful than he, and that he does not fully understand. At another he is a schemer and manipulator, even at the very last when he is very old and blind, crossing his hands over in order to bless the younger of Joseph's sons before the older.

The Two Brothers

The supremacy of the second-born or younger son is a constant motif in the Bible. In the first pages of Genesis Abel the second son is more virtuous than Cain. Moses, the towering figure of the Book of Exodus, and the supreme 'teacher' in Jewish tradition, is himself a second son, his brother, Aaron, being the older. Isaac, as we have seen, is preferred to Ishmael. And this theme dominates the early chapters of the Jacob story. Rebecca, like the other matriarchs, Sarah before her, and Rachel after her, was initially barren. The birth of her children was in itself, therefore, something of a wonder. But she had so much pain in her pregnancy that she wished that she had never asked for children in the first place. She went 'to enquire of the Lord' (Genesis 25:22) to ascertain the cause of her distress. Since the rabbis believed that God did not speak to women, except to Sarah, they interpreted this verse to mean that she went to the House of Study that had been established by Shem. There she was told that she was carrying twins, 'two nations . . . and the older shall serve the younger.'

The younger, of course, was Jacob, and the older Esau. The struggle between the two brothers, already evident in the womb, was a prefigurement of the continuing battle between their descendants. Esau was the ancestor of Edom, otherwise known as Seir, and Edom was a bitter enemy of Israel. Furthermore, in later Jewish tradition, Edom became a symbol for Rome, the most ardent persecutors of the Jews and of Judaism in the first two centuries CE, and intermittently thereafter. And when the Roman Empire adopted Christianity as its official religion Edom (and with it Esau) came to represent the Church. It is not therefore difficult to understand the ignominy that is heaped upon Esau and Edom in Jewish legend. The rabbis could not openly attack Rome or the Church. The consequences would have been disastrous and probably fatal, not only to the perpetrators of the attack but to their communities as well. Therefore they resorted to vilifying the symbols of their oppressors.

For example, the struggle between the two babies in the womb was explained like this. Whenever Rebecca passed by an idolatrous shrine Esau struggled to get out, to participate in the devotions there; and whenever she drew near the Jewish House of Study Jacob tried to force his way out in order to devote himself as early as possible to the study of Torah (*Genesis Rabbah* 67). Other legends maintain that they were already quarrelling over the birthright. Esau did not believe in a future world of spiritual bliss. Jacob therefore agreed that Esau could have the material, terrestrial world of this life, as long as he could take possession of the world to come.

When Rebecca's difficult pregnancy came to an end it was Esau who emerged from the womb first. He was so anxious to be the first that in his eagerness he gave no thought to his mother's welfare, and inflicted a wound upon her that prevented her from having other children. Indeed, God would not have permitted Esau to be born first at all. It was only out of consideration for Rebecca's health that it was allowed. Otherwise she might have died (*Midrash ha-Gadol* I, 434). Esau was hairy (*sair*) all over, and also of a very ruddy (*adom*) complexion. This explains the two names for the nation that descended from him: Seir and Edom. So unusual was his appearance that Isaac did not think it advisable to circumcise him at the prescribed age of eight days, in case the baby died. He thought it preferable to wait until he was thirteen, which was the age of Ishmael when he was circumcised. But by that time Esau had decided that he would not be circumcised, and he never was (*Hadar Zekenim* on Genesis 25:25). (Hence neither the Romans nor the Christians practise circumcision.) Jacob in contrast was born already circumcised.

The Birthright

The contrast between the two brothers was also evident in their daily lives. Esau followed the tradition of the pagan Nimrod and became a hunter, while Jacob stayed indoors, studying at the Academy of Shem and Eber. The famous account of the sale of the birthright to Jacob, and the deceit practised by Jacob and his mother, Rebecca, on Isaac in order to gain the old man's blessing have caused the rabbis great soul searching. Jacob is shown up very unfavourably in the scriptural narrative. Although later interpretation does not try to conceal or ignore the moral dilemma posed by these passages, extenuating circumstances are proposed that serve to justify them.

As far as the sale of the birthright is concerned, stress is laid on Esau's impetuosity in striking the bargain, and his utter dismissal of the importance of the birthright. This is brought out in the actual style of the Bible with its string of five finite verbs: 'Esau ate, drank, arose, went away, and despised his birthright' (Genesis 25:34). Furthermore, Esau had just come in from hunting, an expedition on which he had actually killed Nimrod, and he was so full of his own exploits that he had forgotten that his father was in mourning for Abraham, who had just died. We know this because Jacob was cooking lentils (the famous 'red pottage'), and it is a Jewish custom to eat lentils during a period of mourning, for the round shape of the lentil symbolises the birth-death cycle of human life. Esau was so uncouth that he had no respect for the feelings of his family at that time (*Baba Batra* 16b).

On the other hand, Esau is portrayed in the Bible as having great filial piety. He looked after his father's physical needs, and he was after all Isaac's favourite. Therefore, says the midrash, Esau's descendants were rewarded in this world, the Romans and the Christians having far greater physical power than the descendants of Jacob.

The Blessing

Rebecca was not directly involved in the sale of the birthright, but in obtaining Isaac's blessing she was the actual instigator. Of the four matriarchs she seems to have had the most forceful character, compensating perhaps for Isaac's relative weakness. It was her plan that Jacob should impersonate his older brother in order to gain his father's death-bed benediction, and it was her idea too that Jacob should drape his arms in sheepskin so that when the blind Isaac felt him he would be duped into thinking that his arms were the rough arms of Esau.

Perhaps we may digress here a moment to speculate on the reasons for Isaac's blindness. For the rabbis old age was not a sufficient explanation for such a misfortune to befall one of the patriarchs. They therefore suggested that his incapacity could be traced back to the Akedah. The angels wept to see him bound upon the altar waiting for Abraham's knife to fall, and their tears fell into Isaac's eyes causing his blindness. Another view is that Isaac, seemingly about to die, was accorded a premature vision of the presence of God (the Shekhinah) in heaven, and he was literally blinded by such a resplendent sight (*Genesis Rabbah* 65).

The drama of the blind Isaac being deceived by Jacob, and then being confronted by his real first-born Esau, is one of the greatest stories in world literature, and it is told in the Bible with superb narrative skill. The author plays on the reader's anticipation. During the whole of Isaac's conversation with Jacob the reader knows that the identical scene has to be re-enacted with Esau. Esau is a pathetic character, and his plaintive cry 'Have you only one blessing, father? Bless me, even me, also' is a great tragic moment.

We know now from contemporary ancient Near Eastern literature that the first-born did not receive the paternal blessing as an automatic right. The father could bestow it on whichever child he chose. This seems to be the background reflected in the original story. But by the time it was retold in the Bible the author was living in a society where the first-born did have a pre-emptive right to the blessing. And so the episode of Jacob's and Rebecca's deception was evolved in order to explain the unexpected outcome. A rational analysis of the story, however, cannot match its dramatic impact. The author portrays with a few deft strokes Isaac's terror when he realises he has been caught up in the rivalry of the two sons, and has unwittingly thrown his weight behind Jacob, and the intensity of the narration is increased by the well-worn but never-failing device of the close proximity of events: 'No sooner had Jacob left his father than Esau his brother came in' (Genesis 27:30).

It is a moot point, however, whether the rabbis of a later age had a purely literary appreciation of Scripture. The stories in the Bible were useful as pointers to moral truths or to later historical events which concerned the whole Jewish people, but were consistently regarded as less important than the precise and detailed laws in the Torah. Consequently, even such a magnificent narrative as this was not appreciated for its own intrinsic merits, but only in so far as it could throw light on other things. Perhaps the most significant aspect of the traditional interpretation is that Isaac knew that it was Jacob he was blessing. He realised this from the fact that Jacob had used the name of God when he said 'God has prospered my way' – a phrase which would not have come easily to Esau's lips. Furthermore, the smell of Jacob's garments was the smell of paradise, not the smell of the field where Esau hunted (*Genesis Rabbah* 65). And then Isaac specifically states, 'The voice is the voice of Jacob, but the hands are the hands of Esau.' This sentence, incidentally, was interpreted in typical rabbinic fashion to mean that as long as the voice of Jacob can be heard in prayer and study the hands of Esau can have no power over him. In other words, while Jews are faithful in the practice of their religion they will not be overcome by their enemies.

The hostility of Esau towards Jacob increased, and Jacob therefore had to escape from him. In addition, Isaac and Rebecca were both tormented by the idolatrous practices of Esau's wives and they insisted that Jacob should travel to their ancestral home in Haran to find a wife from among their own family.

'With only a single staff' did Jacob cross the Jordan, and this implies that he journeyed in great poverty. Some later interpreters blamed Isaac for sending his son away with insufficient means. Others say that Jacob had set out with considerable riches but that he had been pursued by Esau and his men who had robbed him on the way (*Genesis Rabbah* 68).

Bethel

The first vision that Jacob had of God occurred on this journey. A good example of the way in which Jewish legends can be derived from a precise exegesis of the actual words of Scripture can be seen here. The Biblical text (Genesis 28:11) says that Jacob came to *the* place, not to *a* place. The spot is not identified. But clearly to the rabbis it was the one and only place, that is, the site of the Temple, the very spot where Jacob's father had suffered the tribulations of the Akedah. Another example of this detailed examination of the text is the conclusion drawn from the fact that in one verse (28:11) it says that Jacob took 'of the stones of the place and put [them] under his head' as a pillow. But later (28:18) it says that 'he took the stone that he had put under his head, and set it up as a pillar'. Obviously, a transformation had occurred. Several stones had during the night become one stone! There are two explanations offered of this phenomenon. One is that Jacob took twelve stones, representing his future sons, and also the tribes of Israel, to see whether they would be united into a single people. The single stone that appeared in the morning confirmed his hopes. The second story is that before Jacob lay down to sleep all the stones of the place vied with each other for the honour of being the pillow on which the great patriarch would rest his head. To settle the quarrel God turned all the separate stones into one single stone (Rashi).

During his sleep Jacob was accorded a vision of the ladder that stretched up to heaven. He saw the angels that had accompanied him hitherto going up to the celestial regions, and a 'relief' team of angels coming down. He also saw on the ladder the four great empires that were later to have such a mighty impact on the history of Israel: namely, the Babylonian, the Persian, the Greek, and the Roman (*Leviticus Rabbah* 29:2). But the most important part of the vision was the divine promise that had previously been given to Abraham and Isaac and was now given for the first time to their descendant Jacob. 'I shall give you and your seed the land on which you lie' (Genesis 28:13). 'Is that all?' asks the rabbinic interpreter in astonishment. Of course not. By a miracle the whole expanse of the Holy Land became contracted for a brief moment into just the area that was covered by Jacob's sleeping body (Rashi). And anyway, the next verse says that Jacob's descendants will spread in all directions of the compass – a much larger area than was promised either to his father or grandfather! A rather uncomplimentary phrase is the divine statement that Jacob's children shall be 'like the dust of the earth'. The meaning is clear, however, with the hindsight of history. The more you tread upon the Jewish people the more they will rise up and make themselves known – just like the dust of the earth.

Rachel and Leah

The account of Jacob's love for Rachel is the earliest romance in Jewish literature. 'Jacob served seven years for Rachel, and they

seemed just a few days to him, because of the love he felt for her'
(Genesis 29:20). It is important to see with what skill the narrator
weaves this story into the whole saga of Jacob's career. Laban is
presented in the Bible in a very bad light, and even more criticism is
heaped upon him in rabbinical literature. But the deceit Laban
practises upon Jacob in giving him his oldest daughter Leah to
marry instead of Rachel is portrayed as a kind of come-uppance for
Jacob's own ruse against Esau. When Jacob protests at the treatment
that he has received Laban taunts him with, 'It is not done in our
circles to give the younger daughter precedence over the first-born'
(29:26). In the midrash Leah also reminds Jacob of his own
questionable past. When after their wedding-night Jacob upbraids
her for answering to the name of Rachel, she says, 'That is exactly
what you did when your father Isaac asked you: Are you my first-
born Esau?' (*Genesis Rabbah* 70).

Incidentally Leah is described in the Bible as having 'tender' eyes.
The Hebrew word is ambiguous. It can mean 'beautiful', implying
that this was her one and only mark of beauty, whereas Rachel was
entirely 'of beautiful form and fair to look upon', (Genesis 29:17).
Or it can mean 'weak'. In which case, the reason for her disability,
according to a rabbinic idea, was that she had been told that being
the older she was to marry Esau, Isaac's first-born. This prospect
filled her with such terror that she wept continually, thus impairing
her sight (Rashi).

The Jewish custom of the bride's circling the bridegroom seven
times before the wedding ceremony is often associated with the
Jacob story. The bridegroom ensures that it is his real intended that
he is about to marry and not another.

All Jacob's children were born while he was in Laban's employ,
except for one, Benjamin. Rachel died just after giving birth to
Benjamin. She wanted to call him Benoni (son of my affliction), but
Jacob named him Benjamin (son of the right hand). Rachel's death,
and especially her burial in Ephrath, instead of in the patriarchal
resting-place in Machpelah, were seen by the rabbis as a punishment
for the fact that she had stolen her father's household gods, the
terafim. We now know from ancient Hurrian texts that the
household gods gave their possessor first claim on the family
inheritance. Rachel was, therefore, acting in the best interests of her
husband and his children. But the rabbis were not to know this.

Indeed, the Biblical narrator does not seem to have known it either. The only excuse that the midrash can give for Rachel's action is that she was trying to wean her father away from idolatry. Jacob was later to destroy these figurines and bury them in Shechem (Genesis 35:4).

Jacob's departure from Laban, his return to Canaan, and his reconciliation with Esau form the setting for his dramatic confrontation with a supernatural being at Jabbok ford (Genesis 32:23 ff). The identity of this being has been the object of conjecture for centuries. In Genesis he is simply called *ish* (a man), but it is clear that he is no ordinary human being. Modern interpreters have seen the story as a representation of Jacob's struggle with himself: it is the crucial phase in his own personal development. The 'man' is his own conscience, reminding him of the deceit he has practised on his brother, Esau. By his victory in this nocturnal wrestling-match Jacob comes to terms with his past. He emerges bruised from the conflict but with a new 'persona'. He is no longer to be called Jacob, the deceiver, but Israel, a prince of God.

Older Jewish commentators have seen the struggle as a conflict between Jacob and Esau's guardian-angel, Samael, the power of evil. The fact that Jacob's adversary begs him to let him go because dawn is breaking is sufficient evidence to suggest that we are here dealing with a creature of darkness, which would suit this identification admirably.

But a very common midrashic view is that Jacob's opponent was none other than the angel Michael, who was later to become the guardian-angel of Jacob's descendants, the House of Israel. Michael was anxious to return to heaven before the sun rose so that he could join the angelic ranks as they sang praises to their God. Jacob first wrested a blessing from him, namely, that his name would be changed to Israel 'because you have struggled with men and with God and have prevailed', the word Israel meaning 'he who struggles with God'. An understanding of this name is, of course, extremely important for the Jew. It is his divine designation, and it is not surprising that it has received many interpretations, ranging from 'he who has seen God' (*ish ra'ah el*) to 'God's remnant' (*she'ar el*). They can all be justified by later Jewish historical experience, but perhaps the original derivation – the man who struggles with God – is still the most profound and apposite, since the Jews' relationship with God has never been easy. The Jews for their part have often been faithless and have had to rely on the divine forgiveness. On the other hand, they have also at times been perplexed by God's apparent neglect of his own chosen ones; and the maintenance of faith has not always been easy.

JOSEPH

J ACOB BECOMES reconciled with Esau, and thereafter Esau and his family appear only fitfully upon the scene, although, of course, his descendants in the shape of the arch-persecutors of the Jews figure frequently in the midrashic literature.

We move from a consideration of the personality and experiences of Jacob to that of the history of his sons. The great saga of the sons of Jacob – that is, of Joseph and his brothers – is the most detailed narrative in the Pentateuch. It is told with consummate artistic skill. The various themes are interwoven with subtlety and dramatic irony. The climaxes are measured in superb fashion. And throughout we have the pivotal figure of Jacob who looks back to the divine promises made to his father and grandfather and also forward to the Israelite sojourn in Egypt, and the dramatic events that flowed therefrom. The story is one of family and personal intrigue, of rivalries and jealousies, but also of brotherly affection and trust. And at the same time the action appears to be part of an inexorable divinely-planned destiny. Although the name of God occurs less frequently here than in other parts of the Pentateuch, his presence is felt throughout moving as it were behind the scenes, and occasionally coming suddenly to the fore, as when Joseph disclaims any personal ability to interpret Pharaoh's dreams. 'It is not in me. God will give Pharaoh an answer of peace' (Genesis 41:16); or when Joseph comforts his brothers and pleads with them not to feel guilty, because 'it was not you that sent me here, but God' (45:8).

The Biblical story of Joseph is more full of detail than any of the other narratives we have treated so far, and one might therefore suppose that there would be less scope for later legendary additions and interpolations. But this is not the case. The more detailed the story, the more leads there are for the imagination to work on. The description in Genesis of Joseph's youth tells us that he used to tell tales about his brothers: 'he brought evil report of them to his father' (37:2). What was this evil report? He accused them of entertaining licentious intentions towards the daughters of the Canaanites, and of transgressing the prohibition of eating the flesh of a living animal (one of the Noachid laws). He also spent a great deal of his time attending to his personal appearance. That is why he is described as 'being still a lad'. He would be very particular about his hairstyle, and he even used eye makeup (Rashi). In fact, throughout the midrash concerning Joseph great stress is laid on his physical beauty. This was prompted by the story of his attempted seduction by Potiphar's wife, and also by Jacob's blessing: 'Joseph is a fruitful vine, a fruitful vine by a fountain. Its branches run over the wall' (49:22). The Hebrew of this verse is obscure and lends itself to many different interpretations. The last few words are sometimes explained as 'the daughters [of Egypt] would climb on the walls' in order to gaze at the beauty of Joseph as he passed by.

Joseph sold into Egypt

Jacob naturally loved Joseph more than his other children because he was the son of his favourite wife, Rachel; and he usually liked to keep him at home. It was with some foreboding therefore that he sent him far afield to see how his brothers were faring. Jacob, however, had been reassured by the dreams that Joseph had had. These dreams had made his brothers jealous and they hated him for what they considered to be his precocious presumption. But Jacob, although outwardly angry with him, 'kept the thing' in his heart, because he had had personal experience of dreams in which God had spoken to him, and he saw Joseph as his successor in that regard.

Joseph set off on his father's instructions to Shechem. But his brothers were not there, and he did not know which way to turn, until he met a certain 'man', who told him where his brothers were pasturing their sheep. This 'man' is a mysterious figure. He plays an absolutely crucial part in the story, for had he not been there to direct Joseph, Joseph would not have been seized by his brothers and sold into Egypt. The whole later history of Israel would have been completely different! So it is not surprising that efforts were made by later rabbinic scholars to identify him. It was noted that the same word *ish* (man) is used of the strange creature who wrestled with

Jacob at the ford of Jabbok, and since he was identified with an angel, here too a divine being is presupposed, namely, the angel, Gabriel (*Pirke de-Rabbi Eliezer* 38).

The brothers saw him coming dressed in the special tunic that his father had made for him. It is traditionally translated as 'a coat of many colours', but we have no real linguistic grounds for accepting such a translation. Other renderings of the Hebrew are 'a cloak reaching to the ground' or 'a cloak heavily embroidered'. At any rate, the sight of this beautiful garment incensed his brothers even more, and they resolved to do away with him. The Biblical narrative at this point is a little confused. It is clear that the original plan to kill him was thwarted by the oldest brother, Reuben, and that it was Judah who then conceived the idea of selling him. But how was the transaction actually effected? No fewer than three groups of merchants are mentioned: Ishmaelites, who appear on the horizon and prompt Judah's plan in the first place; Midianites, who drag Joseph out of the pit, and sell Joseph to the Ishmaelites; and Medanites, who sell Joseph to Potiphar in Egypt. Some modern scholars maintain that here we have a mixture of more than one narrative tradition, and that perhaps the Medanites and the Midianites are the same, a slight scribal discrepancy having crept in. The midrashic explanations follow the Biblical narrative in all its details: the Midianites take Joseph out of the pit, and sell him to the Ishmaelites. On their way down to Egypt the Ishmaelites meet the Medanites, descendants of Abraham, and they sell Joseph to these Medanites, who in turn sell him to Potiphar.

Joseph, the Chaste

The ravishing beauty of Joseph's appearance excited the passions of Potiphar's wife. He was the most handsome man in Egypt. He exuded a wonderfully sweet fragrance that permeated the whole land, so that all that the noble ladies of Egypt had to do was to follow their noses and they could then have the inestimable pleasure of gazing on him (*Midrash Shir ha-Shirim* 3a). No wonder that Potiphar's wife, who was continually in his presence, became so enamoured of him. Joseph, however, remained chaste. He resisted all her advances, and she became literally sick of love for him. Once when her companions enquired as to the cause of her illness she invited them all to a banquet, and put on the tables in front of them some oranges, and knives with which to eat them. She then ordered Joseph to appear before them. The ladies were peeling their oranges but could not take their eyes off him, with the result that they cut their hands so badly that the blood flowed. (*Sefer ha-Yashar*, *Vayeshev* 87a–b). Traces of a similar story may be found in the Koran (12:31).

Joseph nearly gave in to temptation. It was an important festival day in Egypt, and everyone had gone down to the River Nile to celebrate, so that 'there was none of the men of the house there' (Genesis: 39:11). Potiphar's wife had excused herself on grounds of illness, and when she was alone with Joseph she exercised all her wiles upon him. He was about to succumb when he suddenly saw his father's image at the window. Jacob told him that in time to come the names of all his sons would be engraved on the stones of the High Priest's breastplate. 'If you commit this sin,' he said, 'you will be known as "one who keeps company with harlots" [Proverbs 29:3]. Do you want your name to be obliterated?' This gave Joseph pause, and he once again rejected his would-be seducer. (*Sotah* 36b).

She in turn became an implacable enemy and accused him falsely of attempting to violate her. Potiphar therefore had him thrown into prison. Joseph became in later tradition the symbol of chastity and sexual fidelity. He is often referred to as Yoseph ha-Tsaddik (Joseph, the Righteous). In Kabbalah, which sees all the patriarchs as symbols of the sefirot, that is, aspects of the divine attributes, often portrayed as parts of the body of Primeval Adam, Joseph represents *Yesod*, otherwise the male genital organ which channels the flow of beneficient influence to the Shekhinah.

A remarkable fact in the Biblical story is that Pharaoh 'gave him in marriage to Asenath, the daughter of Poti-phera, priest of On' (Genesis 41:45). Is it possible that Joseph could have married the daughter of the very woman who had tried to seduce him, and, moreover, the offspring of a pagan priest? Could Joseph's children, Ephraim and Manasseh, and all their holy descendants trace their lineage back to this unworthy Egyptian family? Clearly not. Asenath was, in fact, the daughter of Joseph's half-sister Dinah. When she was born Jacob put an amulet round her neck engraved with the words 'Holy to the Lord'. The angel Gabriel carried her to Egypt and brought her to the home of Poti-phera. Since his wife was barren, Poti-phera decided to adopt the baby girl as their own. So it was that Joseph married a member of his own family (marriage between uncle and niece being permitted in Jewish law). (*Pirke de Rabbi Eliezer* 38.)

While he was in prison Joseph encountered Pharaoh's butler and baker, and interpreted their dreams for them. These dreams had more than one significance. Joseph saw in them not only the meanings that he gave, but also other meanings that referred to the history of Israel, and these he kept to himself. For example, the butler dreamt of a vine which had three branches. The vine was Israel, and the three branches Moses, Aaron, and Miriam; and the whole dream was about the redemption of Israel from Egyptian slavery. Similarly, the three baskets of bread that the baker saw in his dream symbolised the three major powers that had oppressed Israel, and the birds eating the bread represented the destruction of these powers (*Genesis Rabbah* 88:5–6).

Joseph, the interpreter of dreams, soon became known to Pharaoh, and once he had exercised his art in interpreting the dreams of this mighty ruler, he was appointed vizier of the land, with sole responsibility for preparing for the famine which he had foreseen.

The Reconciliation

The stage is now set for the reconciliation of Joseph with his brothers and his reunion with his father, Jacob. The description of these events is without parallel in the Bible for its depth of pathos, and its portrayal of deepest human emotions. The brothers confront unknowingly the man they had earlier plotted to kill. Only Joseph (and the reader) understand the real situation. On the brothers' second descent into Egypt, this time with Benjamin, the tension is heightened even further. The simplicity of the narrative style highlights the mixed and harrowing feelings that sweep over Joseph. His first question concerns his father: 'Is your father well, the old man of whom you spoke? Is he still alive?' (Genesis 43:27). And then he sees the youngest brother, and has to ask whether this is indeed Benjamin. On receiving an affirmative reply he just has time to pronounce a blessing over him ('May God be gracious to you, my son') before he breaks down, unable to keep up the pretence any longer. 'Joseph made haste; for his heart yearned towards his brother; and he looked for somewhere to weep; and he went to his room, and wept there. Then he washed his face, and came out again.' But still the time had not come for the final disclosure. The tension is maintained until to his brothers' utter astonishment and terror, Joseph simply says, 'I am Joseph. Is my father still alive? . . . Come near, I pray you. . . . I am Joseph, your brother, whom you sold into Egypt.'

No midrashic elaboration can 'improve' on the dramatic force of this episode. Rabbinic interpreters filled out the characters of the individual brothers, emphasised with one of their favourite methods how 'measure for measure' was effected, the brothers suffering in the same way that they intended Joseph to suffer. But in this case the story is best left to speak for itself.

Jacob, the old and ailing father, now has to be told of the rediscovery of Joseph. The Bible once more relates this in the simplest manner possible. 'They told him: Joseph is still alive, and he is ruler over the whole land of Egypt' (Genesis 45:26). At first Jacob could not believe them. But when they offer proof he says with the minimum of words: 'It is enough. Joseph, my son, is still alive. I will go and see him before I die.' A midrash points out that the brothers would not have broached the news so abruptly in case their father died of shock. As it was, 'his heart fainted' and he had to be revived. They therefore asked Serah, the daughter of Asher, to begin to prepare Jacob for the news. She was an accomplished musician, and sang gently to the harp, mouthing the words that Joseph was still alive. It is a common rabbinic view that the holy spirit cannot reside in a place of sorrow. And so when, for example, a prophet is bereaved or has suffered some other misfortune his ability to prophesy is temporarily removed from him. So it was with Jacob. The Shekhinah, the divine presence, had not been with him since the day of Joseph's disappearance. When, however, he heard Serah's sweet tones he felt the holy spirit revive gradually within him, and so he was prepared for the glad tidings when they came. (*Sefer ha-Yashar, Va-yiggash*, 109b–110a).

Jacob went down into Egypt with his whole family, seventy in number. Thus began the sojourn of the Israelites in a land which was later to be the land of bondage, and from which they would emerge as a nation with a divine destiny. The aged patriarch made the express wish not to be buried in Egypt, and he asked Joseph to promise to take his coffin up to the Holy Land (Genesis 47:30). Jacob knew that the resurrection of the righteous would take place there, when the Messiah came, and he did not relish the thought of a journey underground from Egypt to Canaan before being resurrected (Rashi).

Before his death Jacob blessed Joseph's sons, Ephraim and Manasseh. Although Joseph placed his first-born Manasseh at Jacob's right hand so that he might receive the blessing appropriate to the first-born son, Jacob crossed his hands over, so that it was Ephraim who was blessed first. Right to the very end Jacob, though ill and blind, was a master of intrigue. The reason, however, for the specific blessing of these two grandsons was to ensure that the Holy Land should be divided up into twelve shares, one for each tribe. Levi, the priestly tribe, was not to have a territorial portion at all. Consequently, one of the twelve had to have two shares. This was to be Joseph, whose two sons took a share each.

When the aged patriarch died Joseph placed his body on a couch of ivory, which was plated with gold, studded with precious stones, and surrounded with linen and purple hangings. Jacob's sons poured spiced wine around the body, and burnt incense by its side. In attendance were the chiefs of the house of Esau, and the rulers of the house of Ishmael. Judah proposed that a cedar should be planted at the head of Jacob's grave, 'for', he said, 'from him twelve tribes shall arise; and priests wih their trumpets; and levites singing to their stringed intruments.' Joseph simply fell upon Jacob's face, and wept over him, and kissed him. (*Targum Yerushalmi*.)

Joseph obeyed his father's last wish, and with a large escort of brothers and of Egyptian nobility, took Jacob's body to the cave of Machpelah, the burying-place of the patriarchs (Genesis: 50:13). And when his turn to die came Joseph also left a request that his 'bones should be carried up from here' (50:25). This request was fulfilled by Moses. The midrash states that Joseph's coffin in the meantime was placed in the Nile. The *Zohar* maintains that this was done by his brothers so that the Egyptians should not worship his body. Other authorities say that it was done by the Egyptians on the advice of their sorcerers, who tried to hide the body because they knew that the Hebrews could never leave Egypt without it.

It was Moses himself who fulfilled the pledge of taking Joseph's coffin out of Egypt. Serah, Asher's daughter, told him that it was in the Nile, but Moses did not know how to raise it. In the end he used Joseph's own silver divining cup. He cut four pieces from it. On one he engraved a lion, on another an eagle, on the third a bull, and on the fourth a man. He threw the first one into the river, imploring Joseph to appear 'because the time has arrived for the redemption of Israel'. But nothing happened. He was equally unsuccessful with the second and third. But after he had thrown the fourth piece of the cup into the water, and had made the same plea, Joseph's coffin floated to the surface, Moses took it, and it accompanied the Israelites on their long journey to the Promised Land (*Midrash ha-Gadol* I 886–7).

MOSES

Egypt and Sinai

WITH THE Book of Exodus the story of the Jewish people enters a completely new phase. One might indeed say that Genesis is a prologue to the great events that are to take place in Egypt, and between Egypt and the Promised Land. The patriarchal narratives contain the prehistory of the Hebrew people, emphasise the promises that are later to be fulfilled, and introduce the ancestors not only of the Jews but of the other nations in the ancient world who are going to play such a large part in their development.

The stories of Abraham, Isaac and Jacob illustrate the first communication in Israelite history between man and the one God. But, apart from the divine pledges concerning their descendants, the patriarchs' experiences remain on the personal, local level. With Exodus we move from the plane of the individual to that of nations. The Jewish people here emerge on to the stage of history. The family of Jacob that has moved freely into the land of Goshen becomes enslaved. A nation is formed in bondage. Their liberation – the exodus – is their first taste of independence. And while they are still homeless they receive the impress of the divine charge. They commit themselves to fulfil God's commandments, revealed to them at Mount Sinai. With this responsibility upon their shoulders, this burden that was later referred to as 'the yoke of the kingdom of heaven', they move towards the Promised Land.

The very fact that the birth of the Jewish people was inextricably bound up with the experience of slavery made a very deep impression on the later development of Judaism. In the Bible itself it is cited as a fundamental reason for correct moral conduct: 'You shall love [the stranger] as yourself, because you were a stranger in the land of Egypt' (Leviticus 19:34). The exodus is recalled at every conceivable opportunity in Jewish religious life. On the eve of the Sabbath, for example, when *Kiddush** is recited over wine, the head of the household recalls not only the creation of the world – when God rested on the seventh day – but also designates the Sabbath 'as a memorial of the exodus from Egypt'. And, of course, the whole cataclysmic event is narrated in detail and with great celebration on the Festival of Passover. Every year at this time the Jew is enjoined to act 'as if he had just come out of Egypt', and for many Jews in the long and painful saga of Jewish history not much imagination was required.

Release from imposed subjection to a foreign tyrant was swiftly followed by self-commitment to the divine will. The experience of the Hebrew people at Sinai where they received the Torah, the instructions of God himself, again left an indelible impression. All later religious ideas and practices are derived, either directly or indirectly, from this Torah. Indeed the word 'Torah' became synonymous with Judaism itself, and to study and fulfil the Torah is the supreme goal of the traditional Jew.

Naturally, therefore, the legends that surround these two critical moments – the exodus from Egypt, and the revelation at Sinai – are very numerous and varied. Many of them concern Moses, the principal figure in both events. If he had played a leading role in just one of them he would have been assured of a place in world history. But to lead the Jews out of Egypt and, in addition, to bring them the Torah from Mount Sinai, should surely have crowned him with eternal glory. Judaism does not glorify its heroes, however, and no exception is made for Moses. He is revered, of course; but not in his own right, only as the servant of God. His good qualities are praised: his courage, perseverance, humility, and concern for the weakest among his people. At the same time his faults are not overlooked: especially his short-temper and impatience. Because of his failings he was not allowed to enter the Promised Land. He died on the 'wrong' side of the Jordan, and the Bible tells us that no man knows where he is buried; in order, add the rabbis, that the people should not turn his grave into a shrine.

Perhaps it is because Judaism's two daughter-religions, Christianity and Islam, focus so much attention on the personalities

*A prayer for the sanctification of a holy day.

associated with their origin that Judaism plays down the role that Moses had in the foundation of its faith. In the *Haggadah*, the book which is used on Passover-eve, and which relates the events of the exodus, Moses is not even mentioned. To God alone is the glory given. Moses is not a hero. His name is, however, given the most honourable epithet that Jews can bestow. He is *Mosheh rabbenu*, 'Moses, our teacher'.

Enslavement

The express reason for the enslavement of the Hebrews in Egypt was that they were considered by the 'new Pharaoh' to be a foreign body who might ally themselves with an enemy attacking from without. They were also becoming very numerous. Jacob and his household were seventy in number when they went down to Egypt. But when the Israelites emerged into freedom there were six hundred thousand of them! Pharaoh consequently decided not only to remove their liberty but also to decrease their fecundity by the simple method of killing all their male children soon after birth. The Bible tells us that he entrusted two Hebrew midwives with this murderous task. They are named as Shiphrah and Puah (Exodus 1:15), whom a midrash identifies as Jochebed, the mother of Moses, and Miriam, his sister. They, of course, refused to carry out his wishes, and when Pharaoh demanded to know why, they replied that the Hebrew womenfolk had their babies quite naturally, and did not need midwives. And so they did not know when the children were born. (*Sotah* 11b).

Pharaoh therefore decided on a new plan. He would search for the Hebrew boys and throw them into the river. He thought that God would not punish him in the same way, because he had sworn not to destroy mankind again with a flood. But he did not realise that that promise applied to the whole human race, not to any one part of it. So Pharaoh's hosts were destroyed in the waters of the Red Sea. It was a case of exact retribution: measure for measure (*Exodus Rabbah* 1:22). To forestall the Jews' attempt to hide their babies, the Egyptians took their own babies with them when they searched the houses. The Egyptian children cried, and the Hebrew babies would cry in sympathy and so betray their presence.

An extraordinary story is told in *Sotah* 11b of how God looked after the children of his people. 'When they were about to give birth the Hebrew women would go out into the field and have their children under the apple-trees. God would send someone from heaven to help them in their labour. When the babies were born, he would take two pebbles. From one the baby sucked oil and from the other honey. When the Egyptians discovered them they would come after them, but God wrought a great miracle. He made the earth swallow the children. The Egyptians then brought oxen and tried to plough them up, but to no avail. After a time they arose like grass from the ground, and returned in great numbers to their homes. These were the first to recognise the work of God at the Red Sea, saying, "This is my God and I shall glorify him,"' because they had already experienced his saving power.

Moses' Youth

Moses' parents were Amram and Jochebed. Amram was not only a Levite, but also the head of the Sanhedrin, and therefore he set an example to the other Jews in Egypt. When he heard of Pharaoh's evil decree, he resolved to have no more children, and ceased having conjugal relations with his wife. The other Jews followed his example. His daughter, Miriam, however, showed him the folly of his decision. 'Pharaoh has condemned the boy-babies,' she said, 'but you have condemned both the boys and the girls. Pharaoh's decree may not be carried out, but because you are righteous and so highly thought of, your conduct will be imitated everywhere.' Amram saw the wisdom of his daughter's reasoning. He resumed living with his wife, and Moses was born (*Exodus Rabbah* 1:17).

Similar stories are told about Moses' early days as are recounted about Noah and Abraham. The place where he was born became filled with a celestial light; he began to walk and talk immediately; and in Moses' case he started to eat adult food right away. His exposure to risk and danger in his little ark of bulrushes is not only part of a common motif in many heroic stories, but also recalls the binding of Isaac. In the earlier story it is the angel of God himself who protects the child, but here it is Moses' sister, Miriam, who stands watch to see that he comes to no harm (Exodus 2:4).

The romantic account of his rescue by none other than a princess of the Egyptian royal house almost brings a touch of faery into the otherwise grim and relentless struggle which is about to confront Moses. And yet the Bible itself does not seize the opportunity to expand on his childhood and upbringing in the Egyptian court. It was left to rabbis – and modern critical scholars – to do that. Some of the latter go so far as to suggest that Moses was an Egyptian prince by birth. They point to the fact that his name is the Egyptian equivalent of the Hebrew *ben*, meaning 'son of', as in the Pharaonic names Thut-moses, and Ra-meses. In their view, the story of his rescue from the water was an attempt by the Biblical author to derive the name (in Hebrew, *Mosheh*) from the verb *mashah*, which means 'to draw out' of the water (Exodus 2:10). However, there is no need for such a drastic reconsideration of accepted tradition, for even if 'Moses' is Egyptian it could still be the name given by an Egyptian princess to a Hebrew child. To suppose that Moses was not originally a Hebrew at all raises more problems than it solves.

No such problems, of course, worried the Jewish interpreters of the text. They tried to fill in the missing years at court by recounting stories of the effect Moses had on his new environment. One of the most popular of these legends tells of how the baby Moses, being fondled by Pharaoh, seized the royal crown from his head and put it on himself. The court were aghast, and Pharaoh was advised to kill this child who obviously had such overweening ambition. But Jethro suggested that the baby be put to a test, to see whether he acted with intent or not. Two objects were brought on a tray before him: a golden dish on one side and a burning coal on the other. If Moses stretched out his hand to the dish then his previous act was a conscious one. Otherwise it could be disregarded. The young child attracted by the shimmering gold began to put out his hand to take it, but the angel Gabriel knocked his hand to one side, and Moses picked up the burning coal instead. And so he was saved. But this was not all, because just like a baby, Moses immediately put the coal to his mouth and burnt his lips. That is why later he had a speech impediment, being 'slow of speech and of a slow tongue' (Exodus 4:10; *Exodus Rabbah* 1:31).

Moses' Marriage

Moses' discovery of his own Hebrew identity is told very briefly in the Bible: 'he went out to his brethren, and looked upon their burdens' (Exodus 2:11). His passionate anger, which was to prove one of his dominant characteristics in subsequent events, caused him to kill one of the Egyptians. This deed obviously worried later interpreters because they went out of their way to show that Moses knew that the Egyptian had violated the wife of the Hebrew slave whom he was striking; that he also foresaw that the Egyptian was not destined to have any righteous descendants; and that he first enquired of the minstering angels whether the Egyptian deserved to be put to death, or not (*Exodus Rabbah* 1:33).

His deed was witnessed by two of his brethren, identified in the midrash as Dathan and Abiram who were later to cause Moses so much trouble, and he was forced to flee. His long absence from Egypt is the cause of much speculation in Jewish sources. On the basis of Numbers 12:1 which states that Moses 'had married a Cushite woman' a whole story evolved to the effect that Moses was embroiled in a war between the Ethiopians and the Egyptians, and that he was appointed general of the Ethiopian forces. After their victory he became the King of Ethiopia (Ginzberg II, 283–9).

The Biblical story, however, is that he journeyed to Midian, and there married Zipporah, the daughter of Jethro, a pagan priest. This Jethro, the midrash tells us, later became a convert to Judaism, since he proclaimed, 'Now I know that the Lord is greater than all gods,' and offered sacrifice to the God of the Hebrews (Exodus 18:11–12).

The circumstances of Moses' wooing and marriage to Zipporah are similar to those of Jacob's meeting with Rachel, and of Eliezer's encounter with Rebecca. In all these a well provides the focus, and Moses displays his strength just as Jacob did earlier. According to one story the shepherds had actually thrown Jethro's daughters into the well, and Moses had to drag them out of the water. Is this story another attempt to derive the name 'Mosheh' from the Hebrew verb meaning 'to draw out'? (*Exodus Rabbah* 1:38.)

The *Midrash Vayosha* gives us more details of Moses' marriage to Zipporah. In this midrash Moses speaks in the first person and relates how Jethro tested him by asking him to uproot a tree from his garden. This tree was originally the rod which God had created on the eve of the first Sabbath. God gave it to Adam and it was passed on to the patriarchs and had finally found its way with Jacob's family into Egypt. There it had come into the possession of Jethro, who was one of the advisers at Pharaoh's court. Jethro had taken it home and planted it. To Jethro's amazement Moses did as he was asked, and the priest realised that this was the man who was to rescue the Hebrew people from Egypt. He therefore threw Moses into a pit. Zipporah cunningly managed to keep him alive by giving him food in secret. This lasted for seven years. At the end of that time she reminded her father of the man he had cast into the pit. 'Either take his corpse out because of the stench,' she said, 'or, if he is still alive, you will know that he must be perfectly righteous.' Jethro had to be reminded of his name, but when he called Moses, Moses responded. 'He pulled me out,' continues Moses, the narrator, 'and kissed me on the head, and said: "Blessed is God who has preserved you in this pit for seven years. I now believe that it is he that kills and revives the dead, and that you are perfectly righteous. . . ." He then gave me much wealth, and his daughter Zipporah to wed. And we agreed that of any children born in his house, half should be brought up as Jews and half as Egyptians.'

This last statement serves to explain why it happened that one of Moses' sons was not circumcised. The strange story in Exodus (4:24 ff) of how God sought to kill Moses, and how Zipporah saved him by circumcising their son, is explained in this midrash in a curious fashion. Satan in the guise of a serpent met the family as they were returning to Egypt, and began to swallow Moses head first. He was, however, forced to stop when he came to the sign of the Abrahamic covenant. Zipporah immediately understood that the reason for the attack was Moses' neglect to circumcise their second son, Eliezer. She performed the rite herself, and so saved her husband.

The Mission

Moses, again like Jacob before him, had been working as a shepherd for his father-in-law. And it was while he was searching for a stray lamb that he was confronted with the awesome vision of the burning bush. The midrash points out that it was when God noticed the care that Moses expended on his flock that he decided he was a fit man to lead the Hebrew people. The thorn-bush is the most lowly of all nature's trees, and Rabbi Joshua ben Korha pointed out that God selected this bush to show that there is no place so humble that it cannot be the abode of the divine presence (*Exodus Rabbah* 2:5). In order to avoid alarming Moses who was not used to the divine voice God first of all spoke like his father, Amram. Moses immediately responded, 'Here I am, father.' God then told him he was not his father but, 'I am the God of your father, the God of Abraham, the God of Isaac, and the God of Jacob' (Exodus 3:6). Hence the remarkable fact that Moses' father is mentioned by God in the same breath as the patriarchs.

Moses received the summons to return to Egypt and rescue his people. But he was a reluctant ambassador. In this he was like some of the other prophets who succeeded him. To be the bearer of a divine charge is an awe-inspiring, daunting and often dangerous task. Moses raised not only the objections mentioned in the Bible itself, namely, that the people would not believe him, and that he was an imperfect vehicle for the divine word, but, according to the midrash he also reminded God that he had promised the patriarchs that he himself, and not a human being, would bring the Hebrews out of Egypt. Furthermore, Moses protested, the 400 years of oppression that God had foretold to Abraham had not yet elapsed. Only 210 had gone by since Jacob had descended with his family into Egypt. To both these objections God responded. He promised to care for the Israelite people himself, and he pointed out that the time of oppression had to be dated from the birth of Isaac, and so 400 years had indeed gone by (*Exodus Rabbah* 3:3–4).

Before Pharaoh

The care with which the rabbis studied the Scriptual text is evident in that they noticed that of all the Israelites only Moses and Aaron appeared before Pharaoh, and yet in Exodus 3:18 God says to Moses 'thou shalt come, thou *and the elders of Israel*, to the King of Egypt'. They explained this discrepancy by saying that the elders did set out with Moses and Aaron for the palace, but as they got nearer they became more and more afraid, and they sloped off one by one. God punished them for their lack of faith and courage, and when the Torah was given to Moses on Mount Sinai the elders were not allowed to go up with Moses, who said to them 'Wait here until we come back' (Exodus 24:14). (*Exodus Rabbah* 5:17.)

The dialogue between Moses and Aaron on the one hand and Pharaoh on the other is portrayed in the Bible principally as a conflict concerning the release of the Hebrew slaves. But it is, of course, also God's struggle, a contest by which God can make his power known to succeeding generations. The theological conflict is spelled out quite explicitly by the midrash, which seizes on Pharaoh's simple words, 'Who is the Lord that I should listen to his voice...? I do not know the Lord' (Exodus 5:2), and explains that Pharaoh looked for the name of the God of the Hebrews among his sacred records but could find only such gods as those of Moab, and Ammon, and Sidon.

'"You are looking for a living God among the dead," retorted Moses and Aaron.

'Pharaoh enquired, "Is your God a young or an old man? How old is he? How many cities has he conquered? How many countries has he taken? How long has he reigned?"

'"The power and might of our God fill the world," they replied. "He existed before the world was created, and he will exist at the world's end. It was he that created you and bestowed upon you the spirit of life."

'"What has he done?" asked Pharaoh.

'"He has stretched out the heavens and established the earth. . . . He splits mountains and shatters rocks. . . . He covers the hills with grass. He brings the rains and provides shade. . . . He creates the embryo in its mother's womb, and brings it to birth..."

'"You are liars," exclaimed Pharaoh. "I am the lord of the universe, and I created myself, and the Nile as well."' (*Exodus Rabbah* 5:18.)

This dialogue is clearly aimed at contemporary idolatry, the worship of the ancient gods of Greece and Rome; and it is important to realise that the redemption of Israel from Egypt was not only a matter of liberation from servitude; it was seen by the midrash additionally as a release from a pagan idolatrous environment. Moses had a double task: a physical and a spiritual redemption. The latter was the more difficult, as can be seen from the subsequent history of Israel in the wilderness of Sinai, which included the worship of the Golden Calf.

The plagues which, one after the other, gradually compelled Pharaoh to let the Hebrews go, are the object of much speculation and elaboration in Jewish legend, and we cannot go into all the details here. It is interesting to note, however, that Moses had no hand in three of the plagues. These were instigated by Aaron instead. They were the first three: blood, frogs and lice. The reason given by the midrash is that Moses owed his life to the water and therefore could not be involved in turning the water into blood, or bringing the frogs out of it. As for the lice, these were produced by striking the dust of the ground, and here again the dust had helped Moses in the past by hiding the Egyptian whom he had slain, and so Moses was spared the task of striking it. An amusing sidelight on the plague of frogs is that it helped to settle a border dispute between Egypt and Ethiopia. The frogs covered the whole land of Egypt – but no further. Their presence therefore showed quite plainly the limits of Egyptian territory! (*Exodus Rabbah* 10:2.)

The Exodus

Just before the Exodus the Hebrews celebrated the first Passover, a ceremony which although changed extensively over the centuries is still observed by Jews to this day to commemorate that great event of liberation from bondage. The narration of the story includes a recital of the plagues, and in order to express sorrow for the suffering that they entailed a drop of wine is taken out of the wine cups as each plague is enumerated. The Bible not only describes the first Passover but actually lays down its ordinance for successive generations (Exodus 12:2). So we can say that here we have the first laws given to Israel as a people, as distinct from those given to the patriarchs as individuals, or to mankind as a whole. Little wonder that one rabbi, Rabbi Isaac, declared that the Bible should have begun with this section and not with the account of Creation (Rashi, Genesis 1:1).

The Hebrews left in great haste, not allowing sufficient time for the dough they had kneaded to rise. Hence, the explanation for eating unleavened bread on Passover. They also left with great riches. 'They despoiled the Egyptians' (Exodus 12:36). The midrash tells us that the Egyptians were only too glad to get rid of them, and showered them with gifts. Not that these riches were of benefit to them. On the contrary, they proved a stumbling-block. It was from Egyptian gold that the Golden Calf was fashioned in the wilderness, which is not surprising since the possessions of idolaters will naturally lead to idolatry.

As we have already mentioned the narration of the Exodus story in Jewish homes at Passover does not mention the part played by Moses. It is God who is the sole object of praise. This attitude is strengthened even further by a reading of the crossing of the Red Sea. The miracle that took place there was clearly God's work alone. The elaborations of this episode in later Jewish tradition are many. Not only is it an exciting story in its own right, but the Song of Moses which praises God for his great exploit (Exodus 15) lends itself to extensive interpretation. This song is given a special place in the weekly reading of the Torah in the synagogue. A particular chant has been evolved for its recitation, and it is customary in some communities for the congregation to stand while it is being read.

Exodus Rabbah (23:4) points out that this was the first song of praise that mankind had ever addressed to God. 'Adam did not sing, nor Abraham after being rescued from Nimrod's furnace, nor Isaac after surviving the Akedah, nor Jacob after being delivered from the angel and from Esau.' Furthermore, the women led by Miriam joined in the song too, and, the midrash continues, God prevented the angels from praising him until both the Israelite men and women had finished their song: 'My children come before my servants.' At the Red Sea the most humble female-slave saw more of the divine glory than the great prophet Ezekiel.

According to some traditions, the sea did not divide until the Hebrews had first demonstrated their faith in the divine salvation by wading into the waters. Some credit a member of the tribe of Benjamin with this courageous feat. Others maintain that it was Nahshon, the prince of Judah. According to one view twelve different roads opened up in the sea, one for each of the twelve tribes, and each one with massive walls of sea on either side. But the sea became clear as crystal so that each tribe could see the others crossing over.

Traditions vary as to the fate of Pharaoh. Some maintain that he perished with all his host. Others say that he was saved because at the very end he proclaimed the greatness of God and forswore idolatrous beliefs. He suffered grievously, however, and at the end was installed as king of Nineveh. It was he who believed Jonah's threat of destruction, and called upon his people to repent.

The Torah

The Hebrews were released from Egyptian bondage for a higher purpose than simply to achieve freedom. God's demand was: 'Let my people go, that they may serve me' (Exodus 7:16). The exodus was but a necessary prelude to the total commitment of the Jewish people to the service of God, and this commitment was given by them at Sinai. Here the Torah, God's teaching, was revealed to them through Moses, his prophet, and thenceforth the Torah became the solid foundation of Jewish religious life.

The stories and legends extolling the virtues of the Torah, and the prophetic and rabbinic exhortations to the people to remain faithful to it are innumerable. The Torah takes second place only to God himself in the veneration and respect accorded to it. It is the source of light and life. It is the vehicle through which man can approach God and indeed imitate his ways. By observing the commandments of the Torah the Jews are able to hasten the time of redemption and the establishment of God's Kingdom on earth. Equally, neglect of the Torah and failure to fulfil its precepts bring in their train suffering and disaster.

We have already seen that the midrash regards the Torah as having existed potentially before the creation of the world. In fact, God is portrayed as consulting the Torah before embarking on the act of creation. The revelation of the Torah at Sinai, therefore, was simply a communication to mankind of a source of wisdom, a code of conduct, which pre-existed man himself. This concept is borne out, in the rabbinic view, by the fact that long before the revelation at Sinai the patriarchs had observed at least some of the precepts contained in the Torah. A few commandments had already been explicitly stated: Adam had been instructed 'to bear fruit and multiply', and Abraham to circumcise his sons. But implicitly too, it was pointed out, the patriarchs had kept the commandments. Abraham had 'loved the stranger' by providing hospitality to the three angels. Joseph had observed the prohibition against committing adultery by resisting the seductive advances of Potiphar's wife. (Jellinek, *Beth ha-Midrash* VI 40–41.) And such examples could be multiplied.

Furthermore, God began to give the Hebrews a taste of the Torah before they actually arrived at Sinai. After they had crossed the Red Sea they came to a place called Marah, where the water was too bitter for them to drink (Exodus 15:23 ff). The people lodged one of their frequent complaints against Moses, who on God's instructions threw a certain tree into the water, and the water became sweet. What the actual tree was the Bible does not tell us. But a midrash says that it was none other than the Torah, which is 'a tree of life to all those who cling to it' (Proverbs 3:18). This view is supported by the fact that the Bible goes on to say that at Marah 'God made for them a statue and an ordinance' – a foretaste of the Torah. These statutes, the rabbis declared, concerned the Sabbath and honouring one's parents (*Targum Pseudo-Jonathan*).

The regulations were also obviously in force when the miracle of the manna began, because the Bible tells us that 'on the sixth day . . . it will be twice as much. . . . See that the Lord has given you the Sabbath; therefore he gives you on the sixth day the bread of two days' (Exodus 16). This was because it was forbidden to leave one's house on the Sabbath in order to gather food. As a reminder of this event Jews still today have two loaves (*challot*) on the table for the Sabbath meal on Friday evening. The challot are covered by a Sabbath cloth, to recall the fact that dew covered the manna when it fell in the wilderness.

The full revelation of the law did not take place until the people had assembled at Mount Sinai, and there they 'perceived the thunderings, and the lightnings, and the voice of the trumpet, and the mountain smoking' (Exodus 20:15). This was a corporate experience, shared not only by the Hebrews but also by 'the mixed multitude' of non-Jews who had come out with them from Egypt. Judah Halevi, a twelfth-century Jewish philosopher, wrote that the Torah must be the very word of God because six hundred thousand people actually witnessed the revelation at Sinai.

It was here that the special bond was forged between God and the Jewish people. A covenant was drawn up and a pact agreed. The Jews were to have the special responsibility of bearing witness to God's existence and of carrying out his commandments. The relationship was not one of 'most favoured nation'. The fact that the Jews were chosen does not imply any automatic pre-eminence over other nations. It signifies only a special role in the world, a particular task. This point is emphasised in the rabbinic interpretations of the great event at Sinai.

'The Torah was given publicly and openly, in a place to which no one had any claim. For if it had been given in the land of Israel, the nations of the world could have said: We have no portion in it. Therefore it was given in the wilderness, publicly and openly, and in a place to which no one had any claim. Everyone who desires to accept it, let him come and accept it.' (*Mekilta Yitro*.)

Although the Torah is written in Hebrew, God actually declaimed it at Sinai in seventy different languages, at one and the same time, so that all the inhabitants of the world could hear it and accept it (*Shabbat* 88b). But they did not do so. When they were asked whether they would obey God's law they enquired as to its contents. One by one they refused. The descendants of Esau said that they could not live by the commandment 'Thou shalt not kill', and the descendants of Ishmael could not promise to observe the precept 'Thou shalt not steal', and all the other nations hesitated in a similar way. Israel was the last nation left, but they did not ask first what the law contained. They immediately replied, 'We shall observe it'. (*Sifre Deuteronomy*.) Their eagerness to agree to the divine offer is explained by the story that God suspended Mount Sinai over them like a basket, and made as if to bury them underneath it if they did not immediately accept his law (*Avodah Zarah* 2b). This idea that Israel accepted the law only under duress gives added meaning to the common phrase 'the yoke of the Torah'.

In a beautiful portrayal of the revelation of the Torah *Exodus Rabbah* 29:9 describes how the whole natural world was conscious of this awe-inspiring moment. 'When God revealed the Torah, no bird sang, no fowl beat its wings, no ox bellowed, the angels did not sing their songs of praise, the sea did not roar, no creature uttered a sound; the world was silent and still waiting for the echoless divine voice which proclaimed: I am the Lord, thy God.'

This last sentence forms the opening of the Ten Commandments. The general view is that the whole people heard the divine voice proclaiming the Ten Commandments, but there is a contrary idea that they heard only the first two and that they were then so overcome with terror that they pleaded with Moses to be their sole representative, so that God could communicate the rest of the commandments through him (*Makkot* 24a).

In the Hebrew scroll from which Jews read the weekly portions of the Torah in the synagogue some of the letters are decorated with little 'crowns', called *taggin*. The Talmud relates that when Moses went up to heaven he saw God putting these taggin on the letters himself. Moses asked him what he was doing. God replied, 'In time to come a man will arise who will interpret these taggin and suspend mountains upon mountains of laws from each one.' 'I should like to see this man,' said Moses. God granted him his request and sat him in the eighteenth row of the disciples listening to Rabbi Akiva, one of the greatest teachers of the law in the second century CE. Moses did not understand what Rabbi Akiva was saying, and did not even recognise Akiva's presentation of the law as bearing any resemblance to the one he had received from God at Mount Sinai. He was therefore very upset. He was consoled by the fact that when Rabbi Akiva was asked by a student the source of his authority he replied, 'It all goes back to the law that Moses received at Sinai.' The story ends on a very sober note. Moses asked to see how the great scholar Akiva would be rewarded. God thereupon showed him Akiva being tortured by the Romans. Moses protested, but God reprimanded him: 'Be silent. Such is my decree.' (*Menahot* 29b.)

This last story, of course, begins in legend and ends in historical fact. Many rabbis (and many ordinary Jews and Jewesses) were martyred for their beliefs by the Romans. For these Jews the Torah was more important than life. Rabbi Hanina ben Teradion was asked by the Romans why he spent so long studying the Torah. 'It is because God has commanded it,' he said. They sentenced him to be burnt at the stake. 'He was wrapped in a scroll of the Torah, and bundles of willow wood were heaped around him, and set on fire. . . . His disciples said to him, "What do you see?" He replied, "The sheets of the scroll are being burnt, but the letters are flying up to heaven."' (*Avodah Zarah* 17b.)

In Rabbi Hanina's view the letters of the law could not be destroyed. Rabbi Akiva, too, had no doubts about the all-demanding nature of the Torah. When asked why he risked death in order to study and teach the Torah, he told a famous parable. 'There was once a fox walking by the side of a stream. He saw some fishes moving hurriedly through the water. He said, "What are you running away from?" They replied, "From fishermen who have nets." "Why do you not come up on the dry land?" the cunning fox suggested, "and we can live in peace together." "If we are afraid while we are in our element," they retorted, "how much more afraid should we be if we left our element!" So it is with us, said Rabbi Akiva. We run risks while we sit and study Torah, which is described as "Thy life and the length of thy days" [Deuteronomy 30:20]. What greater risks we would run if we neglected the Torah.' (*Berakhot* 61b.)

That Moses remained on Mount Sinai forty days and forty nights gave rise to the idea that he must have gone up to heaven to receive the Torah, because only in heaven could he have survived for so long without food and drink. The rabbinic view is that there is no eating or drinking in heaven. The angels do not need it. The angels firmly resisted Moses' attempt to take the Torah away, maintaining that it belonged with them in the celestial spheres. Moses, however, persuaded them by force of argument that mankind needed the Torah more than they did.

'It is written in the Torah, he said, "I am the Lord who brought you out of the land of Egypt." Were you enslaved in Egypt? It is also written "Honour your father and mother." Do you have parents that you need such a commandment? It is also written "Thou shalt not commit adultery." Are there any women in heaven that you need a prohibition like this?' He went on through the commandments until the angels conceded the justice of his argument, and allowed him to take the Torah away. (*Pesikta Rabbati.*)

It is a fundamental part of orthodox Jewish belief that the Pentateuch (i.e. the Torah in its narrowest sense) was dictated verbatim by God to Moses. Every word of it is therefore true and unalterable. Modern critical scholarship does not accept this view, pointing out some inconsistencies in the text, a few anachronisms, and the indisputable fact that the Pentateuch describes Moses' death, adding that 'no man knows of his burial-place down to this day' (Deuteronomy 34:6). There are rabbinic counter-arguments for all the criticisms of modern academics. Even the last point can be answered, for although some medieval rabbis conceded that the verses describing Moses' death were in fact written down by his successor Joshua, there is also an older midrashic view proposing that Moses did himself write down these verses at God's dictation, and that he wept when he was told to describe his own departure from the world!

In addition to the Torah that Moses wrote down, God gave him another Torah which he communicated by word of mouth only, and this oral Torah Moses handed down accurately to his successors. This oral Torah was a commentary on and an expansion of the written one, and was later committed to writing in the *Mishnah* (200 CE). During the forty days, therefore, that Moses spent in heaven he had to devote himself assiduously to learning God's law. The midrash says that he spent the days studying the written Torah and the nights familiarising himself with the oral Torah.

Although the rabbis did not dispute the divine origin of the Torah, the privilege and duty of interpreting it belonged to man alone. Even the prophetic spirit, in the view of the rabbis, ceased with Malachi, and they were suspicious of claims to divine communication. This is illustrated by a very famous story in the *Talmud (Baba Metsia* 59b). Rabbi Eliezer and the sages were arguing about the ritual cleanliness of Akhnai's oven. Rabbi Eliezer declared it to be clean, but they thought otherwise.

'Rabbi Eliezer said to them, "If I am right, let this carob-tree prove it." The carob-tree uprooted itself and moved a hundred cubits. Some say, four hundred cubits.

'They said to him, "You can't prove anything from a carob-tree." Rabbi Eliezer said to them, "If I am right let this stream prove it." The stream started to flow backwards.

'They said to him, "You can't prove anything from a stream."

'Rabbi Eliezer said to them, "If I am right, let the walls of this schoolroom prove it." The walls started to fall. Rabbi Joshua arose and rebuked them saying, "Scholars are arguing here. What business is it of yours?" The walls stopped falling, out of respect for Rabbi Joshua. But out of respect for Rabbi Eliezer they did not straighten up either, and they are still bent over to this day!

'Rabbi Eliezer then said, "If I am right, let it be proved from heaven." A voice from heaven proclaimed, "Rabbi Eliezer is always right." Rabbi Joshua got to his feet and said "[The commandment] is not in heaven" [Deuteronomy 30:12].

'What did he mean by that? Rabbi Jeremiah said, "He meant that since the Torah has been given on Mount Sinai, we no longer pay any heed to a voice from heaven . . ."

'Afterwards Rabbi Nathan met Elijah. He asked him what God did at that time.

'Elijah replied, "He smiled, and said: My children have defeated me. My children have defeated me."'

The Golden Calf

The most common image of Moses accepting the Torah both in the Jewish and Christian pictorial tradition represents him receiving two tablets of stone on which are engraved the Ten Commandments. Moses, however, was so incensed by the sight of the Hebrews worshipping the golden calf that he refused to give these commandments to the people and smashed the tablets. It would seem that the Hebrews could not be weaned away so easily from the idolatry that they had witnessed in Egypt, and, believing that Moses would not come back to them, they demanded a substitute figure who would go before them. The actual Biblical details are slightly ambiguous. The people gathered round Aaron and ordered him to 'make us a god who shall go before us; for as for this Moses, the man that brought us up out of the land of Egypt, we know not what is become of him' (Exodus 32:1). Were they asking Aaron to make them a physical image of a god, or a representative of Moses? Or was their sin that they thought of Moses as a god in human form? Or did they desire a *god* to lead them, because in their view 'the *man*' that had brought them out of Egypt had failed them? Aaron's part in the affair also needs explanation. Why did he give in to their demands so readily? Did he have no faith that his brother would return?

The rabbis in interpreting the story naturally tried to exculpate Aaron, the first High Priest of the Jewish people, who could not in their view possibly fall into the grave error of manufacturing an idol. They maintained that in appearing to accede to the people's request he was simply playing for time. This is shown by the fact that Aaron announced 'Tomorrow shall be a feast to the Lord.' Furthermore, the midrash maintains, Aaron thought that by asking the people for their gold with which to make the calf he would discourage them, and they would desist. He was amazed at their eagerness to surrender their riches. In order to show that they were demanding a foolish and iniquitous thing he threw their gold into a fire. He was surprised at the result: 'I cast it into the fire, and out came this calf' (Exodus 32:24). Aaron himself made the excuse that it was none of his doing!

When Moses witnessed his people dancing round the golden calf his reaction on smashing the tablets of stone was not simply one of anger. He knew that they had already transgressed the prohibition against idolatry, and were liable to be punished with death. Therefore, he thought, it were better not to give them the commandments at all. Some traditions state that as Moses drew nearer to the Israelite camp, he saw that the writing on the stone tablets was beginning to fade, and it eventually vanished altogether, and so he realised that there was no point in giving them to the people.

This first pair of stone tablets was created by God himself. According to *Mishnah Avot* 5:6, they were created on the eve of the very first Sabbath, while the *Zohar* (I, 131b) states that they were hewn from the foundation-stone at the centre of the world. Others say that they were made of the sapphire that is beneath the divine Throne of Glory. The second set, however, were hewn by Moses at God's command (Exodus 34:1). When he descended the mountain with the second set of tablets his face shone, or, more literally, 'beamed'. Rays of light were emitted from his skin. This seems to be the meaning of Exodus 34:30. It was a reflection of the divine radiance, according to rabbinic interpretation. In some representations of Moses, the most well known being the sculpture by Michelangelo, he is depicted as having horns growing out of his forehead. This is a misunderstanding of the scriptural verse.

Tabernacle and Temple

A large part of the Book of Exodus is taken up with the construction of the Tabernacle in the wilderness. This description is paralleled in its detail and complexity only by the account of the building of Solomon's Temple in the First Book of Kings. The gods of the ancient world all had their particular 'homes'. These were temples, shrines, natural groves or streams, or even specific areas in individual houses. The Israelites were, therefore, in the mainstream of ancient Near Eastern religion in constructing an abode for their own God. However, one of the major differences was that any representation of their God was forbidden. There could be no image, or idol. Consequently, the central focus of the temple or shrine could not be, as in most pagan sacred places, a sculptured image of some kind. Their place was taken by the Ark of the Covenant, which in essence was a simple rectangular portable chest that contained the stone tablets of the law. Above the Ark were two sculpted cherubim with wings outstretched; not, of course, a representation of the deity, but a throne on which the unseen God was thought to rest. There are many representations in other ancient religions of divine figures standing on sculpted animals who are meant to be their thrones. The idea of God resting between or over the cherubim may be considered in this light. This concept of the invisible God meant that the physical focus of the sanctuary had to be the Ark, containing the divine law. And this is still the case today, nearly two thousand years after the Temple was destroyed: the central feature of the synagogue is the Ark which contains the sacred scrolls of the Torah, the divine law.

But could God have a physical 'home' on earth at all? Solomon posed the problem better than any one: 'Will God in very truth dwell on earth? Behold, heaven and the heaven of heavens cannot contain thee. How much less this house that I have built!' (I Kings 8:27). The rabbis summarised the position even more pithily: 'God is the place of the world. The world is not his place.' In fact, the midrash tells us that originally it was not God's wish that a sanctuary should be built for him. He only acceded to the demands of the people. When they expressed the wish to build God a palace, like the kings on earth, God replied: 'My children, earthly kings need this, but I do not. I have no need for food and drink. And as for light, the sun and moon are my servants and they illumine the whole world with the light that I gave them.' The people, however, insisted. God then agreed saying, 'It is customary for a father to care for his son, wash him, feed him and carry him, and then for the son, when he is grown up, to provide his father with a room, a table and a candlestick. When you were young, I provided for you, gave you bread to eat and water to drink, and carried you on eagle's wings. Now that you are older, you should provide for me a room, a table and a candlestick' (*Midrash Aggada* Exodus 27:1.)

Of all the appurtenances of the sanctuary it is the 'candlestick', the menorah, that has become the most significant as a symbol of Judaism and the Jewish people. It is found inscribed on ancient Jewish tombs, patterned on early synagogue mosaic floors, and was used as a symbol of national independence on Jewish coinage from Roman times. It is little wonder that the menorah figures prominently among the booty captured by the Romans at the sack of Jerusalem in the year 70 CE and represented on the Arch of Titus in Rome.

The description of the original menorah in the sanctuary is complicated; so much so in fact that the midrash tells us that Moses had great difficulty in remembering all the details. God had given him a plan, a blueprint of the whole tabernacle construction with all its component parts, but Moses had to go back to be reminded of the details of the menorah. God then showed him a replica of fire, but still Moses could not keep all the information in his head. Finally, God told him to give the work to that accomplished artisan, Bezalel, the son of Huri. He made the complete candelabrum out of his own head without even seeing the plan, and it turned out exactly as God had intended (*Numbers Rabbah* 15:9).

The Temple menorah, like the one in the desert-sanctuary before it, had seven lamps. The menorah that Jews use on the festival of *Hanukkah* has nine. This festival which falls in December commemorates the victory of Judah Maccabee over Antiochus IV, called Epiphanes, in 165 BCE. Antiochus had tried to obliterate the Jewish religion by making the practice of it a capital offence, but Judah and his brothers conducted a successful guerilla campaign against the troops of Antiochus, and in the end were able to regain control of the Temple in Jerusalem. They then had to reconsecrate the holy site which Antiochus had polluted with idolatrous worship. There is a legend in the *Talmud* (*Shabbat* 21b) to the effect that when the Maccabees searched for the sacred oil with which to kindle the lights in the Temple they could find only sufficient to last for one day. By a miracle this small amount lasted for eight days until they found the store of oil which had been concealed by the priests during the previous years of oppression. To commemorate this story Jews light the menorah in their homes for eight nights, kindling one candle on the first night, two on the second, and so on, until at the end the whole candelabrum is lit. (The ninth lamp is an extra one called the *shammash*, or 'servant', and is used simply to light the others.)

The garments of the High Priest are also explained in great detail in the Bible, and these descriptions were subjected to intensive scrutiny by later commentators. The panoply of sacrificial worship in the sanctuary and in the Temple must have had inner meaning because communication between man and God is the most mysterious of all religious acts. This was the view particularly of the Jewish mystics for whom all precepts in the Torah were a means by which the Jew on earth could attempt to promote harmony in the celestial spheres. For an example of this type of interpretation let us look at the twelve stones which were in the breastplate worn by the High Priest. Each of them was engraved with the name of one of the twelve tribes. Rabbenu Bahya Ben Asher (d. 1340) in his commentary on Exodus 28, points out that these stones have a close connection with the creation. Each stone in his view bore six letters, representing the six days of creation, and the total number of letters was seventy-two. This figure stands not only for the full seventy-two lettered name of God, but also for the seventy-two hours which it took God to create the world, reckoning each day as twelve hours, since God did not create at night. Then Bahya goes on to interpret each stone one by one. Judah's stone was the emerald, which brings victory in battle, Issachar's was the sapphire, because the tribe of Issachar were well known for their study of the Torah, and the two tablets of stone were hewn out of sapphire. Zebulun was a trader and supported Issachar in his studies. So his stone was the pearl which comes from the sea that was traversed by Zebulun's merchant ships. Reuben's stone was the ruby, which promotes fertility. This is appropriate for Reuben because it was he who, when a lad, found the aphrodisiac mandrake-root and brought it home to his mother, Leah. Other stones are interpreted by Bahya in a similar way.

These stones were also used according to a rabbinic tradition in connection with the mysterious Urim and Thummim, an oracle which was in the charge of the High Priest. When someone came to enquire of this oracle, the High Priest would look at the stones on his breastplate, and the answer would be revealed by certain of the engraved letters shining more brightly than the others.

The hem of the High Priest's robes was decorated with little bells. On only one day of the year did he go into the inner sanctum of the Temple. This was the Day of Atonement, when he would make an offering of incense there. The people in the Temple courts would not be able to see him perform his ministrations because he was shielded from their sight by thick curtains. But they could hear him moving about from the tinkling sound of the bells on his robe. To commemorate this Jews decorate their scrolls of the law with silver bells. The scrolls have silver breastplates too; so that one can say that the role of the High Priest has been symbolically assumed by the *Sefer Torah*.

Exile

The destruction of the first Temple by Nebuchadnezzar in 586 BCE, and the destruction of the second by the Romans in the year 70 CE, were two great national and religious tragedies. Only in the Temple could sacrifices be offered. Therefore its destruction meant an interruption in the ritual communication between man and God. Offerings could no longer be brought, for example, in order to atone for sin. Temple sacrifice on the holy days, as well as the normal daily ritual, ceased. Later tradition tried to find reasons for these catastrophes. Invariably, the blame was laid at the door of the Jews themselves. They had been unfaithful to the Torah. They had relapsed into idolatry. They had failed to educate their children. They had indulged in slander. All these and many more sins were cited which led to national collapse and exile. Indeed, it is only in comparatively recent times that Jews have sought other reasons for their calamities than their own misdeeds.

Legend relates that Moses, the three patriarchs, Rachel, the Torah, and all the individual letters of the Hebrew alphabet tried to intercede with God on the Jews' behalf, begging him to prevent the destruction of the Temple, but all to no avail.

In ancient times the defeat of a nation, and the capture of its sanctuary, invariably meant also the defeat of the national god. This was a concept which could not possibly be related to the situation of the Jews, because the Jewish God is not simply the God of the Jews. He is the God of the whole universe, who uses nations in order to accomplish his purposes. On the other hand, the destruction of the Temple did involve the loss of God's 'home'. This is beautifully expressed in the rabbinic view that when the Jews went into exile, the presence of God, the Shekhinah, accompanied them. The Shekhinah wanders homeless with the Jewish people, and when they suffer, she too suffers. This idea is crucial in Jewish mystical circles, and in all their discussions concerning the goal of Jewish religious observance. This goal is none other than to restore the Shekhinah to her rightful home in the Temple of Jerusalem. The Temple will be rebuilt when the Messiah, son of David, comes. All the Temple furniture, which was hidden away before the destruction, will be revealed once more, and the age-old rituals will recommence.

Giants

The entry of Israel into the Promised Land was delayed for forty years because they believed the majority report of the spies that it was too dangerous a place for them to go (Numbers 13–14). They did not have sufficient faith that God would protect them. Yet it was not surprising that ten of the twelve spies that Moses sent should express their fears for they had seen giants in the land across the Jordan, who were called Anakim. Once when they had visited the city of Kiryath Arba, they saw Anak himself and his three gigantic sons. They were so terrified they hid in what they thought was a cave. It turned out to be a pomegranate skin that one of the giants had thrown away. A woman came by and, picking up the skin with the twelve men inside, threw it to one side as if it were as light as an egg shell. The size of the pomegranate gives us some idea of the fertility of the Holy Land. It was in truth 'a land flowing with milk and honey', and just as beautiful as God himself had promised. The two faithful spies, Caleb and Joshua, insisted on taking back some of the fruit to the Hebrew camp in order to show what a lovely country it was. They cut down a vine, and it was so heavy with fruit that eight men were needed to carry it (*Sotah* 34a). It produced enough wine to supply all the libations for the sanctuary for the next forty years.

While we are considering the nature of the giants we must not overlook Og, King of Bashan, about whom many tales are told. He was supposed to be the son of Ham, and he survived the Flood (see p. 43). His bed was noted in the Bible itself as an object of wonder: 'his bedstead was a bedstead of iron . . . nine cubits was the length, and four cubits the breadth' (Deuteronomy 3:11). From this description it was deduced that Og's waistline measured about half his height! Abba Saul related that he once pursued a stag which escaped into a dead man's thigh bone. He went in after it and chased it for nine miles before he reached the end. The thigh bone later turned out to be Og's (*Niddah* 24b).

The death of Og came about in an extraordinary way. Being so

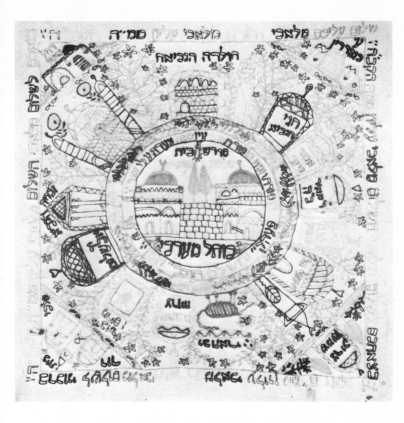

Map of Jerusalem, embroidered in Persian style. Ninteenth century.
Sir Isaac and Lady Wolfson Museum in Hechal Shlomo, Jerusalem.

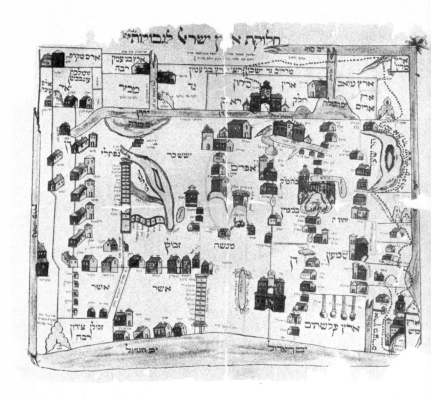

Map of the Holy Land attributed to Elijah, the Gaon of Wilna (1720–1797). The Mediterranean is at the foot, and the dotted line at the right indicates the route taken by the Israelites from Egypt to Canaan. *Jewish National and University Library, Jerusalem. MS Heb. 8° 934.*

David and Goliath. Miscellany. France, thirteenth century.
British Library, London. MS Add. 11639, fol. 523v.

Solomon as Ecclesiastes, the Preacher. Drawing by Ben Shahn, engraved on wood by Stefan Martin.
Ecclesiastes or the Preacher: New York, 1965.

אַדִּיר הוּא יִבְנֶה בֵּיתוֹ בְּקָרוֹב : בִּמְהֵרָה,
בִּמְהֵרָה בְּיָמֵינוּ בְּקָרוֹב · אֵל בְּנֵה אֵל
בְּנֵה · בְּנֵה בֵּיתוֹ בְּקָרוֹב : בָּחוּר הוּא יִבְנֶה, בֵּירָתוֹ
בְּקָרוֹב בִּמְהֵרָה בִּמְהֵרָה בְּיָמֵינוּ בְּקָרוֹב · אֵל בְּנֵה
אֵל בְּנֵה · בְּנֵה בֵּיתוֹ בְּקָרוֹב : גָּדוֹל הוּא · דָּגוּל
הוּא · יִבְנֶה בֵּיתוֹ בְּקָרוֹב · בִּמְהֵרָה בִּמְהֵרָה בְּיָמֵינוּ

The Temple. *Haggadah.* German, 1740.
British Library, London. MS Sloane 3173, fol. 34r.

117

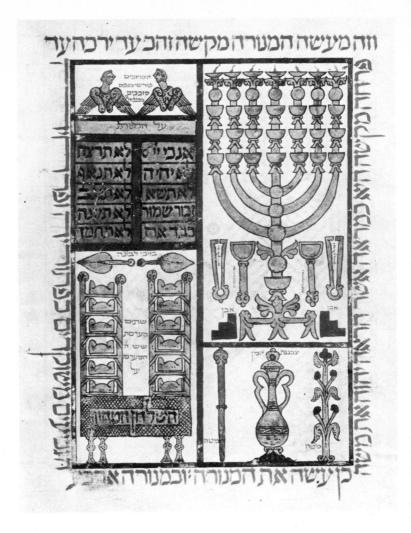

The Temple vessels (note the cherubim at top left). Bible. Spain 1299.
Bibliothèque Nationale, Paris. MS Heb. 7, fol. 12v.

The priesthood of Aaron, with symbols of the Temple. Copy from the mural in Dura-Europos Synagogue. Third century CE.
Yale University Art Gallery, New Haven, Connecticut, Dura Europos Collection.

Adam and Eve, Judith holding the head of Holofernes, and Samson. The woodcut within the text shows Elijah as harbinger of the Messiah. Passover *Haggadah*, Prague, 1526, fol. 23v.
Jewish National and University Library, Jerusalem.

Top Chair of Elijah for rite of circumcision. English, 1809. Formerly in the
Great Synagogue, London.
Jewish Museum, London.

Above Archer executing the sons of Haman. *Megillah*, Kai-Feng-Fu, China,
nineteenth century.

The sons of Haman being hanged. Ardašīr Book. Judeo-Persian, *c* 1650.
Staatsbibliothek, Preussischer Kulturbesitz, Orientabteilung, Berlin. MS Or. qu.
1680, fol. 93r.

מרדכי המן

Haman leading Mordecai, with a woman pouring refuse on Haman from a
balcony. Folk-art. Zawichost, Poland, nineteenth century.
R. Lilientow, 'Święta żydowskie w przeszłości i terazniejszości', Cracow, 1908,
Tab. 18.

Three mythical animals: Leviathan, the wild ox, and the bird *ziv*. Below,
the righteous feasting on the flesh of these animals in the world to come.
Ambrosian Bible, S. German, *c.* 1240.
Biblioteca Ambrosiana, Milan. MS B32, INF, fol. 136.

The entry of the Messiah into Jerusalem. Woodcut by Siegmund Forst.

Ushpizin benedictions. For hanging in the *sukkah*. Paper-cut. Germany,
eighteenth century.
Israel Museum. Jerusalem.

Martyrdom of Hanina ben Teradion. Jerusalem. From the *menorah* of Benno
Elkan.
Photo Yitzhak Amit.

King Ahasuerus seeking a new queen, after deposing Vashti. Ardašīr Book
by Shahin, which contains a poetic account of the Esther story. Persian.
Second half of the seventeenth century.
*Staatsbibliothek, Preussischer Kulturbesitz, Orientabteilung, Berlin MS Or. qu.
1680, fol. 29r.*

tall he could see for a very long distance. Surveying the horizon he perceived the Israelite camp many miles away marching towards him. He calculated that they covered an area of about nine square miles. He therefore picked up a mountain whose based covered exactly the right area and ran towards them intending to cast it upon their heads, and thereby killing them all at once. God, however, frustrated his design. He sent a swarm of rock-eating ants against him. They bored through the mountain so that it fell from his hands and slipped over his neck. He could not remove it, because his teeth jutted out. It was in this parlous state that he encountered Moses. Moses himself was no stripling. He was fifteen feet tall. Moses took a lance fifteen feet long, and jumped fifteen feet into the air, and struck Og on the ankle. Og collapsed, and because of the weight of the mountain round his neck could not rise again. And so he perished. (*Berakhot* 54b.)

Moses' Punishment

The most fateful event that occurred to Moses happened at the waters of Meribah in the wilderness of Zin (Numbers 20). Once more the people complained against him, this time because of their lack of water. This dearth was caused by the death of Miriam, Moses' sister. While she was alive a miraculous well, called 'the well of Miriam' travelled with the Israelites through the desert. It began its journey soon after they had left Egypt and had come to Marah, where the bitter waters were made sweet. As a reward for Miriam's piety, these sweet waters accompanied her everywhere. But when she died they disappeared. The Israelites therefore gathered around Moses demanding water.

Moses appealed to God for help and he was told to speak to the rock which would immediately produce sufficient water for the people. God also told him to take his rod, but did not order him to use it. The Bible tells us that Moses struck the rock twice with the rod and water poured out. This was one of the occasions on which Moses disobeyed God. Furthermore, he ascribed the miracle to himself and to Aaron, saying to the people, 'Listen, you rebels; shall we bring water out of this rock?' (Numbers 20:10). His anger also impelled him to address the people harshly. For these reasons God prevented Moses from entering the Promised Land, saying, 'You did not believe in me, nor sanctify me in the eyes of the children of Israel.' No punishment could have been more painful to Moses than this. Aaron too was punished in the same way because, the midrash says, he failed to stop Moses acting as he did. Other reasons were also advanced by the rabbis for Moses' punishment. One is that he actually denied his Jewish identity. The occasion was long before when he first encountered the daughters of Jethro. They announced his arrival to their father by saying, 'An Egyptian rescued us from the hands of the shepherds' (Exodus 2:19). It may be assumed, therefore, that Moses made himself known to them as an Egyptian and not as a Hebrew (*Deuteronomy Rabbah* 2:8).

Death of Aaron

Of the two brothers Aaron was the first to die. Moses' task on this occasion was to take the priestly garments from Aaron and put them on his son and successor, Eleazar. In order to avoid the unseemliness of Aaron's appearing naked, God covered him with a garment from heaven to replace every garment that was removed by Moses. Others say that Aaron was hidden by a cloud of glory. When Moses and Eleazar came down from Mount Hor, where Aaron had died, the people did not believe that he had departed this life in an innocent and natural way. They thought that perhaps Moses and Eleazar had killed him. In order to quell their suspicions, God commanded the angels to carry Aaron's bier over the heads of the assembled multitude. This demonstrated that Aaron's death was God's will (*Beth ha-Midrash*, I, 95). There is a famous saying in *Mishnah Avot* 1:12, in the name of Hillel: 'Be of the disciples of Aaron, loving peace and pursuing peace, loving mankind and bringing them near to the Torah.' He was much loved by the people, and there are many traditions to the effect that they shed more copious tears for Aaron than for Moses. Moses was at times severe and irascible, although the humblest of all men. Aaron, however, was lovable. Only the men mourned for Moses, it is said, while both men and women mourned for Aaron.

An example of the way in which Aaron promoted peace between man and his fellows concerns a married couple, where the husband was about to divorce his wife. Aaron went to the husband and said, 'If you do divorce your wife, remember that your second wife will almost certainly not be as good to you as this one; for when you have a quarrel with her she will accuse you of being an argumentative type because you divorced your first wife.' Again, he would go in turn to each of two quarrelling parties, and point out to each how very contrite and distressed the other was. In this way, he would bring them together.

Balaam

One of the most curious personalities in the Hebrew Bible is Balaam. Balaam was a heathen prophet and sorcerer with a widespread reputation as a successful miracle-worker. Jewish tradition regards him as one of the magicians and advisers in the court of Pharaoh in Egypt. (Another one, by the way, was Job.) It is one of the ironies of the Jewish liturgy that the verses read or sung at the beginning of the Morning Service were originally spoken by a pagan, Balaam, who came to curse Israel but stayed to bless them, saying: 'How goodly are your tents, O Jacob; your dwelling-places, O Israel' (Numbers 24:5).

Balaam sets out on his ass to curse Israel. On the way they are confronted by an angel with a sword in his hand. But only the ass can see it. And the animal deviates from the path into a field. Balaam beats him, and they resume their journey. Once more the angel appears, at a spot where the road is bounded by a wall on each side. The ass veers and crushes Balaam's foot against the wall. A third time the angel appears, and this time the ass cannot move to right or left, but just sits down on the road, unable to proceed further. Balaam is furious, and strikes his animal several times. The ass thereupon opens its mouth and speaks to Balaam, protesting its innocence. Balaam's 'eyes are opened' and he sees the angel. The lack of any surprise on Balaam's part when his animal speaks gives the impression that this sort of encounter was not uncommon in ancient Near Eastern legend, and we must assume that there were many other stories of this type now lost. The conversation between Eve and the serpent is, of course, another example.

Despite Balaam's enmity towards the Jewish people he is held in high esteem in later Jewish tradition. He occupies the place among the heathen prophets that Moses enjoys among the Hebrews. Indeed, he has some advantages over Moses: 'No prophet has arisen like Moses in Israel, but there has been one among the other nations, namely Balaam. . . . But there is a difference between Moses' prophecy and that of Balaam. Moses did not know who was addressing him, but Balaam knew. . . . Moses did not speak with God till he had stood up, but Balaam spoke with God "fallen down, yet with opened eyes"' (*Sifre Deuteronomy*).

Death of Moses

Moses, having intimations that he was soon to die, was instructed by God to pass on the leadership to Joshua. Joshua had already distinguished himself as one of the two spies who had brought back a good report about the Promised Land. In that incident he is called Hoshea (Numbers 13:8), but his name was later changed to Joshua. This was done partly to accommodate the complaint of the smallest letter of the Hebrew alphabet, the letter *yod*. When Sarai's name was changed to Sarah, the yod was displaced, and the letter protested to God at being removed from the name of the first Hebrew matriarch. God made amends, saying, 'I shall take you from the end of the name of the matriarch, and place you at the very beginning of the name of the leader who will bring Israel into the Promised Land.' Joshua deserved to succeed Moses, because he had for long ministered to him, fulfilling the important and honourable role of serving the most renowned teacher of all. Moses did not, however, fulfil God's command to the letter. He had been told 'to lay your hand' upon Joshua (Numbers 27:18), but when he came to pass on the leadership to him, he in fact used both hands (Deuteronomy 34:9). The result was that he not only conveyed to Joshua his wisdom and understanding of the Torah, but he also passed on to him something of the radiance which was always visible on Moses' face (*Sifre Numbers*).

The time drew near for Moses to die. He appealed to God to grant him a longer life. He appealed to the world of nature and to the patriarchs to intercede for him, but they all replied that they could not influence God for their own benefit, let alone on behalf of someone else. Moses thought to himself that if God wanted him to die in order to make way for Joshua he could step down from the leadership of Israel and show the people that they should obey Joshua's authority and not his. In this way perhaps he could prolong his life. 'Every morning and evening he would minister to Joshua, as a disciple ministers to his master . . . . At midnight he would arise and go to Joshua's door. He would take the key and unlock the door. After entering, he would take a shirt, shake it out, and lay it by his pillow. He would then take his shoes, and clean them and put them by the side of the bed. After this he would take his vest, and his cloak, his golden helmet and his bejewelled crown, examine, clean and polish them, and lay them out in order on a golden chair. He would then fetch a jug of water and a golden bowl and put them in front of the chair – and all this while Joshua was still asleep . . .' But all this was of no avail, because the people could not reconcile themselves to seeing the roles of Moses and Joshua reversed. (Jellinek, *Beth ha-Midrash* I, 123.)

When the last moments came Samael, the angel of death, begged God to let him have the pleasure of removing Moses' soul. After much deliberation God consented, and Samael set off. But he found Moses studying the Torah, and such a resplendent light flashed out of his eyes that Samael was afraid to draw near. Therefore God took upon himself the duty of taking the great man's soul. 'Three angels descended with the Holy One, blessed be he: Michael, Gabriel, and Genael. Gabriel laid out Moses' couch; Michael spread a purple sheet over it; Genael prepared a woollen cushion for a pillow. The Holy One, blessed be he, stood at his head, Genael at his feet, Gabriel at one side and Michael at the other. The Holy One, blessed be he, said, "Cross your legs," and he did so, "Put your hands upon your chest," and he did so. "Close your eyelids," and he did so. Then the Holy One, blessed be he, called to Moses' soul, "I have allotted you one hundred and twenty years in Moses' body. Now come out, do not delay, for your time has arrived to emerge." The soul replied at once, "I know that you are the God of spirits and souls, and that in your hand are the souls of the living and the dead, and that you have created me and formed me and placed me in the body of Moses for one hundred and twenty years. Who else has a body as pure as Moses? I do not wish to leave it . . ." The soul persistently refused to forsake Moses' body of her own accord. In the end, God had to take his soul himself with a kiss, as it is said "Moses, the servant of the Lord, died there in the land of Moab, at the mouth of the Lord"' (Deuteronomy 34:5). (Jellinek, *Beth ha-Midrash*, VI, 77.)

SAUL AND DAVID

Saul

THE FIERCE controversies that regularly took place between king and prophet in Israel began at the very inception of Israelite kingship with the appointment of Saul. According to the Biblical record this appointment indicated a rejection by the people of God's direct leadership through the prophet Samuel. 'They have not rejected you,' God says to Samuel, 'but they have rejected me' (I Samuel 8:7). Subsequently, therefore, all the kings of Israel were judged by their contemporaries and by later ages according to whether they had acted in accordance with the divine law or not. Their political achievements were offset against their moral failings.

According to the midrash it was only after Saul had been anointed king that he began to sin at all. Before that he was as innocent as a new-born baby. This led to his selection, but coupled with this self-commending quality he was tall and handsome, and much beloved of the womenfolk. The Bible itself tells us that 'there was not among the children of Israel a goodlier person than he: from his shoulders and upward he was taller than any of the people' (I Samuel 9:2). He also had an honourable lineage. The tradition does not tell us a great deal about his father, Kish, but his grandfather, Abiel, was remembered for the fact that he introduced public street lighting so that the people could find their way to the houses of study after dark. So Saul benefited from 'the works of the fathers' (*Leviticus Rabbah* 9:2). However, even when Samuel had broken the news to him of his selection, he was so humble and self-effacing that he would not accept the throne until the appointment had been confirmed by the Urim and Thummim on the breastplate of the High Priest.

Saul's greatest sin, as recorded in the Bible, is that he failed to carry out the divine command to exterminate the Amalekites (I Samuel 15: 9 ff). It was because of this that the royal inheritance was taken from Saul's family, and a new king, David, was chosen to succeed him. The fascinating relationship between the young David and the ageing Saul is not elaborated upon overmuch in later Jewish sources, although the picture of the young David playing his harp to Saul in order to lighten his depression is a familiar one in the Western tradition.

The midrashic elucidation of Saul's encounter with the witch of Endor, however, is more detailed. The witch, identified in some sources as Zephaniah, the mother of Abner, did not recognise Saul because he had disguised himself (I Samuel 28:8). But she realised that it was the king who had asked her to raise up the spirit of the dead Samuel, when Samuel appeared at her bidding the right way up. If it had been any other person apart from the king the spirit would have been upside down. Such are the rules of necromancy. Another rule is that the necromancer can see the dead spirit but not hear him, while the enquirer can hear but not see him. That is why Saul had to ask the witch to describe Samuel to him (*Leviticus Rabbah* 26:7).

Samuel's spirit did not arise alone. The ascent of Samuel into the world of men prompted other dead spirits to think that 'the end of days' had arrived, and that the resurrection was about to take place. Moses rose with Samuel, and others too (*Pirke de-Rabbi Eliezer* 33).

Samuel told Saul that it was time for him to make atonement for his sins. And so, on the next day, Saul showing more bravery than his successor David, who was not wont as king to lead his troops into battle, appeared at the head of his army with his three sons. They engaged the Philistines on Mount Gilboa and were all slain. And there is no greater atonement than death.

David's Ancestry

David can lay claim to be the greatest of all the kings of Israel. He is not associated with the royal pomp and splendour that accompany his son, Solomon, in Jewish legend. Nor did he have Solomon's mastery of wisdom. But historically speaking he laid the foundation for the most powerful period of the Jewish monarchy. He captured Jerusalem and made it his capital city. He extended the borders of his domain. And moreover he is linked in the religious literature of the Jews, and in their prayers, with the Messiah; the traditional belief being that either he himself or a descendant of his will come 'at the end of days' to restore the Jewish people to their ancestral glory and inaugurate the Kingdom of God on earth.

His ancestry, however, is not without its problems. There is a genealogy at the end of the Book of Ruth which specifically links David directly with Ruth. Ruth and Boaz had a child named Obed, who is 'the father of Jesse, the father of David' (Ruth 4:17). Ruth was therefore David's great-grandmother. However, she was not a born Israelite. She came from the people of Moab. And there is a Biblical injunction that 'An Ammonite or a Moabite shall not enter into the congregation of the Lord, even to the tenth generation' (Deuteronomy 23:4). If applied strictly this would exclude David! This became the subject of great controversy, and was settled, in the view of the midrash, in David's own time. Doeg, who was constantly hostile to David, maintained that the law affected David. Abner, however, pointed out that the Deuteronomic phraseology was in the masculine form, and referred to males only. Ruth, the Moabitess, was outside the scope of the law, and there was no question but that David, her descendant, had every right to be included in 'the congregation of the Lord'. The prophet Samuel had finally to be summoned to arbitrate between them, and he upheld the view of Abner (*Ruth Rabbah* 2:5).

The kabbalists regarded David's descent from the Moabites as a definite advantage, indeed an absolute necessity. The pagan Moabites represent the 'other side' – the power of uncleanness, or evil – and the future Messiah has to have experience of evil before he can finally overcome it, at the end of time. The Messiah, therefore, in the kabbalistic view, has evil within his very nature, and only through this personal involvement with, and knowledge of, 'the other side' can he restore the world (Joseph Caro,* *Maggid Mesharim*).

In other respects David's lineage was impeccable. A rabbinic tradition maintains that he was descended from Moses' sister, Miriam, who had married Caleb. He therefore had priestly ancestry,

*Rabbi Joseph Caro, 1488–1575. Born Spain and died in Safed. He was both a mystic and the last great codifier of Jewish law.

since Miriam and Moses were of the tribe of Levi. It is clear therefore that the future Messiah would be directly connected both with the priestly line and with the royal house of Judah. (*Sifre Numbers*, 78.)

The Brave Youth

Like Saul before him, David was renowned for his handsome appearance. 'He was ruddy, and withal of beautiful eyes, and goodly to look upon' (I Samuel 16:12). This was not the main feature, however, that commended him for the royal throne of Israel. It was rather the care and courage that he displayed in looking after his father's sheep. In this respect he was like Moses. Both of them impressed God as shepherds. As a shepherd-boy David was fearless. On one day he killed four lions and three bears (17:34) with no weapons except stones from the ground, thus giving earnest of the more famous contest yet to come. His most extraordinary adventure, however, was with the re'em, usually translated in the traditional Bible versions as 'wild ox' but in reality a mythical creature of enormous size and ferocity (see p. 43). On one occasion David mistook the sleeping re'em for a mountain, which he started to climb. The beast suddenly roused itself and David was lifted high in the air on its horns. He prayed to God promising that he would build a Temple as high as those very horns. God listened to his prayer and sent a lion of whom even the re'em was terrified. The huge monster bowed down to the lion, thus enabling David to dismount; and he was saved from the lion, too, because God sent a deer who drew the lion away in pursuit. (*Midrash to Psalms* 22; 91; 92.)

David's most famous exploit, of course, was his conquest of Goliath, the Philistine giant. The Biblical account (I Samuel 17:4–54) is in itself a masterpiece of story-telling, and really requires no elaboration. We see the young boy David bringing provisions for his brothers, picking his way through the ranks of the Israelites and asking apparently in all innocence, but actually with some impudence, what reward the slayer of Goliath would receive from the king. He is reprimanded by his older brother for staying to see the outcome of the battle and neglecting his sheep. 'What have I done?' says David. 'Was it not but a word?' He goes on making enquiries until the attention of Saul is aroused, and David offers himself. Saul brings him his armour, but David cannot wear it, not because it is too large, but because 'he has not tried it'. He was not used to it. He preferred his own shepherd's ways. He taunts Goliath. 'You come to me with a sword, and with a spear and with a javelin. But I come to you in the name of the Lord of hosts, the God of the armies of Israel.' With a single stone from his sling David brings down Goliath and cuts off his head with the giant's own sword.

The Jewish legendary tradition fills out the details of the story, giving us, for example, information about Goliath's pedigree. He was the son of Orpah, the sister and also sister-in-law of David's great-grandmother Ruth. Orpah was as reprehensible as Ruth was virtuous – but an old maxim teaches us that even a wicked person's few good deeds have to be recognised and recorded. Orpah followed her mother for only forty paces; that is why her son Goliath was allowed to taunt Israel for forty days. Orpah shed just four tears when she parted from her mother. Her reward was four sons, all giants, the mightiest of them being Goliath. (*Sotah* 42b.)

The five stones that David chose actually came to him voluntarily. They represented God, Abraham, Isaac, Jacob, and Aaron. These five stones, like those of Jacob at Bethel (see pp. 76–7), miraculously turned themselves into a single stone. And this was the one stone that killed Goliath. (*Midrash to Samuel* 21, 108.)

A Muslim variant story tells of three stones. As David made his way to the battlefield he heard a voice calling to him from the ground. 'Pick me up and put me in your pouch,' it said, 'for I am the stone which Abraham used to drive away Satan.' David picked it up and passed on. Again he heard the voice of a stone saying, 'Pick me up and put me in your pouch because I am the stone upon which the angel Gabriel rested when he made a fountain spring up in the desert for Hagar and Ishmael.' David gathered that one too, and then he heard a third saying, 'Pick me up and put me in your pouch, for I am the stone with which Jacob was victorious in his struggle with the angel.' It was only after he had gathered these stones that he found out about Goliath's challenge. (Rappoport III, 6.)

The Musician

It was David's prowess in this contest that gave him a place in Saul's entourage. At least that is what we are led to believe from one of the

Biblical accounts. But a different one ascribes his place in court not to his courage but to his musical proficiency on the harp. For Saul became subject to what we would probably call today fits of severe depression: 'The spirit of the Lord had departed from Saul, and an evil spirit from the Lord terrified him.' (16:14). He was advised to seek out 'a man who is a skilful player on the harp'. The young David was sent for and his music was found to have soothing, curative properties: 'It came to pass, when the evil spirit from God was upon Saul, that David took the harp and played with his hand; so Saul found relief, and it was well with him, and the evil spirit departed from him.' (I Samuel 16:14; 16:23.)

David as musician, and 'sweet singer in Israel', to whom most of the psalms were attributed, is a much loved figure in Jewish legend. There are many representations of him with his harp in Jewish art from ancient to modern times. One Hellenistic mosaic from Egypt shows him as a kind of Orpheus, surrounded by animals, whom he has obviously attracted with his sweet music. In the Bible itself there are psalms which from their content were thought to have been composed by David at a specific time in his life, particularly during his ongoing conflict with Saul. For example, Psalm 57 is headed '[A Psalm] of David . . . when he fled from Saul, in the cave' and Psalm 59 reads '[A Psalm] of David . . . when Saul sent, and they watched the house to kill him.'

The harp that David used was a very special one. Some say that the strings were made from the gut of the ram that Abraham sacrificed instead of his son, Isaac, on Mount Moriah. And it played at the touch of the wind without David's help. 'A harp hung over David's bed, and at midnight a north wind would blow, and the harp would play on its own. David would then rise at once and study Torah until dawn.' (*Berakhot* 3b.)

David and Bathsheba

The character of David, like those of all the other Biblical heroes, is not completely without reproach. The Bible portrays human beings, not saints. They may be only 'a little lower than the angels', but they are definitely 'lower'. The chink in David's armour was his passion for Bathsheba, the wife of Uriah, the Hittite. Not only did he commit adultery with her, but he subsequently arranged for

Uriah to be put in the front line of battle where he was sure to be killed, so that David could marry his widow. This grave sin was not glossed over in the Bible. Nathan, the prophet, upbraids him in a most telling fashion by relating to him the parable of the wealthy man who stole the poor man's 'little ewe lamb'. David's fury at such injustice is swiftly turned into a self-accusation by Nathan. 'You are the man,' he says (II Samuel 11:2–12:7).

The elaborations of the story provide extenuating circumstances, but none of them tries to remove David's culpability completely. David was at fault at the very beginning, goes one version, because he was the one who arranged the marriage between Bathsheba and the non-Jewish Uriah in the first place. After David had killed Goliath he did not know how to unbuckle the giant's armour in order to cut off his head. Uriah came on the scene and offered to help him if he would promise to give him an Israelite wife – a bargain to which David readily agreed. So it was that Uriah married Bathsheba who had really been destined for David. (Moses Alshekh,* II Samuel 12:13.)

Another account, *Sanhedrin* 107a, presents David's infatuation with Bathsheba as a result of his own presumption. He asked God why it was that when people prayed they addressed him as 'God of Abraham, God of Isaac, and God of Jacob' but not as 'God of David'. God replied it was because the three patriarchs had all been put to the test and had been found faithful. 'Test me,' said David. And God did so. One evening David was on the roof of his palace, and Satan appeared before him in the shape of a bird. The king threw a dart at it. It missed the bird but struck a screen which separated David's house from the adjoining one. The screen fell down and revealed Bathsheba combing her hair. David's passion was aroused, and he failed the test.

In later kabbalah the killing of Uriah is seen as a kind of 'restoration' for the sin of Adam. Uriah is a symbol of the serpent, the embodiment of primal evil. Just as the serpent overcame Adam in Eden, so David in turn is victorious over the serpent. (David is a reincarnation of Adam – primeval man – the letters of the name standing for Adam, David and Messiah.) (*Sefer ha-Peliah*.)

*Moses Alshekh, 1508–1600. Rabbi in both Safed and Damascus, he is most well-known for his homiletical commentary to the Pentateuch.

David's sin had dire consequences, the most grievous being his son Absalom's rebellion, and death. The Talmud adds further tribulations to those recorded in Scripture. David was given the choice of suffering himself or causing his descendants to suffer. To his credit he chose the former, and one day while he was hunting Satan appeared in the form of a deer. David pursued him little realising that he was travelling at speed into the country of the Philistines. There he was sighted by Goliath's brother Ishbi. Swift to take vengeance Ishbi seized David and put him in a wine press. The king would have been crushed to death if the earth beneath him had not sunk slowly at the same rate as the press. At that very moment, too, David's plight came to the attention of his cousin, Abishai. It happened to be a Friday afternoon and Abishai was washing in preparation for the Sabbath. He saw drops of blood in the water, which warned him that something was wrong. And then he heard a dove moaning and plucking out her feathers. Abishai recognised the dove as a symbol of Israel, and realised that David was in peril. He looked for him everywhere but could not find him. So he saddled the king's mount and gave him his head. It immediately transported him to the land of the Philistines. There he met Orpah, the giant's mother, who attacked him, but he slew her.

Ishbi saw Abishai coming. He picked David up from the ground and threw him into the air in such a way that he would fall on Ishbi's spear which was stuck in the ground. Abishai seeing this pronounced the ineffable name of God, and David became suspended midway between heaven and earth. David and Abishai then had a conversation, in which David explained how he came to be in this terrible plight. Abishai told him that he should not have chosen to suffer himself. He was too indispensable to Israel. They thereupon both prayed to God for deliverance. Abishai uttered the Name again. David fell to earth safely, and they both fled, pursued by Ishbi. When the giant, however, found out that his mother was no more his strength failed him, and he was despatched by our two heroes. (*Sanhedrin* 95a.)

David's Death

The dying days of David are overshadowed in the Biblical story by court intrigue. But in later legends the main concern is to establish how a man so dear to God and so pious could die at all. David lived to be seventy years old, the normal allotted span, but even that was a mark of special favour. Those seventy years were sacrificed by Adam from his own life. God had shown him the whole future history of the world and Adam saw that David was destined to live only three hours. He thereupon begged God to take seventy years from his life and give them to David. (Hence Adam lived for only 930 years instead of one thousand.) (*Pirke de-Rabbi Eliezer,* 19.)

God refused to tell David the day of his death, for that is revealed to no man, but he did tell him that he would die on a Sabbath in his seventy-first year. Every Sabbath therefore David spent continuously in studying the Torah for he knew that the Angel of Death could have no power over a man occupied with the Torah. The angel therefore resorted to cunning. 'There was a garden at the rear of David's house. The Angel of Death went there and shook the trees. David got up to investigate the noise. He went down the stairway to the garden, and it collapsed underneath him, and he died.' (*Shabbat* 30a–b.)

He was buried in his own city (I Kings 2:10) but the traditional site of his tomb is on Mount Zion, which has become a place of pilgrimage, notably for Oriental Jews who visit it on *Shavuot* (Pentecost) especially, this being the traditional date of David's death. It is held in reverence also by both Christians and Muslims. There are several stories of miracles performed at David's tomb.

One of them describes how a Muslim Pasha looked into the tomb, and accidentally dropped his bejewelled sword into the depths. Some of his retainers were let down into the tomb by rope in order to recover it, but when each one of them was pulled up he was dead. The Jewish authorities were consulted, and the most pious member of the community, the synagogue beadle, was chosen to descend into the murky depths. He succeeded in retrieving the sword. And he later told the story of how he met down there a dignified old man, who personally handed him the Pasha's sword. As a reward, the Pasha treated the Jewish community of Jerusalem with great beneficence. (*Sha'arei Yerushalayim* 470–75.)

David occupies a privileged position in paradise. On the Day of Judgment, there will be a banquet for the righteous in heaven, when they will all taste the delicious flesh of Leviathan. 'David will say to God, "Master of the Universe, may it be your will that your presence should dwell among us." The Holy One, blessed be he, will accept David's invitation . . . and he will enter with David. All the righteous will stand by their thrones, and the Holy One, blessed be he, will sit upon his throne of glory, and David will sit opposite him, on the throne prepared for him. . . .' After the meal Grace is said, and God invites all the righteous in turn to take the cup of wine and say the blessing over it. Abraham refuses because, he says, 'I had a son [Ishmael] who angered God'. Isaac refuses because the descendants of one of his sons, Esau, destroyed the Temple. Jacob refuses because he married two sisters together, which was later forbidden by the Torah. Moses refuses because he was not permitted to enter the Promised Land, and Joshua because he was not blessed with a son. When David's turn comes he accepts, saying, 'I shall pronounce the blessing, for I am the fit person to do it, as it is written [Psalm 116:13] "I shall raise the cup of salvation, and call upon the name of the Lord."' (Jellinek *Beth ha-Midrash* V, 45–6.)

In the physical world too David lives on as the symbol of the Jewish people and of their glorious future in the Messianic Age. As the refrain of a popular song has it *David, melekh Yisrael, hay, hay, ve-kayyam,* 'David, King of Israel, lives still.'

SOLOMON

THE REIGN of Solomon was one of comparative peace and tranquillity after the struggles which his father David experienced while he set about extending his kingdom. It was also a prelude to the eventual disintegration and collapse of Israel, because after Solomon's death a dispute arose over the inheritance, and the kingdom was divided.

The picture the Bible gives us of Solomon is of a man who was fond of the good things in life: vast and beautiful buildings, fine horses and lovely women. And yet he was also credited with two great and lasting achievements: the contruction of the Temple in Jerusalem, and the acquisition of profound wisdom. The rabbis therefore had an ambivalent attitude towards him. They castigated him for his sensual appetites and praised him for his architectural prowess and great intellect, both of which in different ways he directed towards the worship of God.

Women and Horses

There is an old rabbinic dictim that one should not ask the reason why any one commandment should be observed. It is sufficient that God requires it. All we should do is obey. If we try to establish the purpose of the commandments we might think we can achieve that purpose by other means and so neglect the commandments themselves. That is why the Bible does not usually give reasons. There are, however, exceptions. One of them concerns the injunction that the king should not 'multiply wives to himself, *that his heart turn not away*' (Deuteronomy 17:17). Solomon, however, did marry many 'strange' wives, apart from his concubines, thinking that he would be strong enough too resist their wiles, and that his heart would not be 'turned away'. He was, of course, mistaken. He actually built shrines in Jerusalem for the different gods that his wives worshipped. Had Solomon not thought about the reason behind the prohibition he might never have transgressed it.

His most important marriage politically was with Pharaoh's daughter, because this cemented an alliance which bolstered his kingdom against enemies from the north and east. Legend has it that Solomon loved this wife, Bithiah, more than all the others put together, and she led him into more sins than all the others put together. Their marriage was celebrated on the day that the Temple was finished. She brought with her a thousand musicians from Egypt, each with a different instrument, to play on the wedding night. Over the bed she hung a dark canopy embroidered with diamonds and pearls that gleamed like the stars so that when Solomon awoke he thought it was still night-time and did not rise. In consequence the Temple could not be opened, because he kept the keys under his pillow, and the morning sacrifice could not be offered. This was a grave offence, and because in addition Solomon celebrated his marriage more splendidly than the completion of the Temple, God resolved to destroy the great building. On the wedding-night itself the angel Gabriel came down from heaven and stuck a reed in the Mediterranean Sea. Silt began to congeal around the reed, and this proved to be the foundation of the great city of Rome, whose legions were later to set fire to the Temple. (*Shabbat* 56b.)

Lust for women was not Solomon's only weakness; he loved horses too. The chapter in Deuteronomy we have already quoted also forbids the king to send agents to Egypt to purchase horses 'for as much as the Lord has said to you: You shall no more return that way'. This was another command that Solomon ignored, for 'the horses which Solomon had were brought out of Egypt' (I Kings 10:28). Among his multifarious possessions were 'fourteen hundred chariots and twelve thousand horsemen' and for the horses he had magnificent stables built at Megiddo, whose ruins may still be seen.

Solomon's Wisdom

Although Solomon lived a life of great luxury, he redeemed himself in the eyes of later scholars because when God gave him the free choice of a divine gift he asked for no material blessing at all, but for 'an understanding heart to judge thy people, that I may discern between good and evil' (I Kings 3:9). The request was granted. 'God gave Solomon wisdom and understanding exceeding much ; . . even as the sand that is on the sea-shore. And Solomon's wisdom excelled the wisdom of the east, and all the wisdom of Egypt.' He was wiser than certain sages whose names are known only because they pale into insignificance before the great wisdom of Solomon. 'He was wiser than . . . Ethan the Ezrahite, and Heman, and Calcol, and Darda, the sons of Mahol; and his fame was in all the nations round about.' (5:9–11.) This competition was considerable if we accept a rabbinic identification of these mysterious characters. The first three are equated respectively with Abraham, Moses and Joseph, while Darda stands for the whole generation of the wilderness (*Pesikta de-Rav Kahana* 4:3).

Solomon put his intellectual gifts to work. 'He spoke three thousand proverbs; and his songs were a thousand and five' (I Kings 12). The Bible itself ascribes two books directly to Solomon: Proverbs and the Song of Songs; and a third, Ecclesiastes, was attributed by rabbinic tradition to him, since it styles itself as being the 'words of Koheleth, the son of David, King in Jerusalem' and which other son of David was King in Jerusalem? Solomon wrote these books not for self-glorification, but in order to explain the words of God himself, the Torah that was revealed to Moses on Mount Sinai. Much of God's teaching had remained obscure until Solomon interpreted it. 'To what were the words of the Torah to be compared before the time of Solomon? To a well whose waters were at a great depth, and though cool and fresh could not be drunk by any man, until someone was clever enough to join cords and ropes together so that he could reach the water and drink it. So it was with Solomon. He went from figure to figure, and from subject to subject until he obtained the true sense of the Torah.' (*Song of Songs Rabbah* 1:1.) Solomon's style is full of metaphors and similes, 'figures', and his writings therefore need additional interpretation. The whole of the Song of Songs, which may appear to us to be an anthology of poetry expressing the physical love of man for woman and vice versa, is in truth an allegory of the love that God feels for Israel and Israel for God. Rabbi Akiva was quite convinced of the supreme sanctity of the book. 'All the Writings are holy' he said (and by 'Writings' he meant the Hagiographa – the third and last part of the Bible, after the Pentateuch and the Prophets) 'but the Song of Songs is the Holy of Holies' (*Mishnah Yadayim* 3:5).

Solomon the Judge

The first and immediate result of Solomon's acquisition of wisdom was his judgment in the case of the two harlots who both claimed the same child (I Kings 3:16 ff). The way in which he solved this problem astonished all those who witnessed it, and it laid the foundation for countless stories of Solomon's astuteness. He was frequently summoned to arbitrate in disputes or discover unknown culprits, and his advice invariably led to the triumph of the righteous, and the defeat of the wicked. One such story which also occurs in Muslim tradition, concerns a pious Jew who had come to a foreign place. He was carrying a large sum of money with him, and since the Sabbath was approaching, when it is forbidden to carry money, he looked around for someone trustworthy with whom he could deposit it. He could find no one, and so he decided to dig a hole in the ground and hide it. He was observed by his host who seizing an opportune moment dug the money up and stole it. The Jew was desperate. He suspected his host, but he had no proof. He therefore consulted Solomon, and carried out the advice he received. He went to his host and asked him what he should do. He had buried some money, he said, but he had much more on his person, and he did not know whether to conceal this in the same place. The host, foreseeing an even greater prize, encouraged him to repeat the operation, and he quickly got to the place first and put the money he had stolen back in the ground. The Jew then retrieved his wealth and went on his way. (Gaster, *Exempla* no. 111.)

Solomon was reputed to be able to converse with all living creatures: animals, reptiles and birds, and with both good and evil spirits. In this guise he is particularly renowned in Muslim legend, where he is portrayed as the supreme master of all the spirits or jinn. This idea goes back to the Bible itself where we read that Solomon 'spoke of trees, from the cedar that is in Lebanon to the hyssop that grows out of the wall; he spoke also of beasts, and of birds, and of creeping things, and of fishes' (I Kings 5:13). His speaking *of* trees and animals soon became transmuted by tradition into speaking *to* them. One should not be surprised therefore at legends where birds and beasts carry out Solomon's behests and are used by him to solve human problems, or which give Solomon a judicial role in the animal world.

A man carrying some milk came across a snake who was dying of thirst. 'Give me some of that milk,' said the snake, 'and I will show you great treasure.' The man agreed. After the snake had quenched its thirst it led the man to a rock. 'Lift up the rock,' it said. The man did so, and there was the treasure. But before he could stoop to pick it up, the snake coiled itself round his neck and tried to strangle him. 'Is this the way to repay me?' said the man. 'I am going to kill you,' said the snake, 'for trying to take my treasure away.'

The man suggested they put the controversy before King Solomon, and the snake agreed. After some preliminaries Solomon insisted that the snake uncoil itself, since he said that no one litigant should have an advantage over the other. The snake slid to the floor. 'Now,' said Solomon, 'state your case.' 'I want to kill this man,' responded the snake, because it is written in the Scriptures "Thou shalt bruise man's heel."' Solomon thereupon turned to the man and said, 'In that case you should step on the snake because it is also written that you should bruise the snake's head.' The man did so, and the snake died. (Gaster, *Ma'aseh Book* no. 144.)

One of the most famous of these stories concerns Solomon's encounter with Asmodai, the king of the demons, and the riddle that resulted. Asmodai produced from the earth a two-headed man. Solomon was much taken aback and set about questioning this strange creature. It turned out that he was descended from Cain and lived so far beneath the earth that the journey there would take hundreds of years. In his native land the sun moved across the sky from west to east. But he led a normal life, ploughing, sowing and reaping. Solomon asked that the creature should be returned to the place from which he had come, and he was astonished when Asmodai told him that this could not be done. The two-headed man therefore had to stay.

He married and settled down, and grew very rich. He had seven sons, six of whom resembled their mother, but the seventh had two heads like his father. When the father died the question arose of the inheritance (a very common motif in Solomonic legends). The six 'normal' sons claimed that the inheritance should be divided into seven parts and shared equally. But the seventh son insisted that it should be split into eight portions, and that he should have two of them: one for each head.

Solomon was asked to adjudicate. He did not know what to do. He consulted his court, the Sanhedrin. They deliberated on the matter and then refrained from comment, afraid to give a decision in case Solomon disagreed with them. So Solomon went to the Temple at midnight and prayed to God for guidance. In the morning he ordered the two-headed man to be brought in and said, 'If one head knows what is happening to the other they are one man. If not, they are two.' He had the heads blindfolded, and called for some hot water and old wine. He then poured the hot water and wine on one head. Immediately the man cried out, My lord, the king, we die, we die. We are only one person and not two!'

And so the problem was solved. (Jellinek, *Beth ha-Midrash* IV, 151–2.)

The Queen of Sheba

Solomon's intimacy with the kingdom of the animals and the spirits comes to the fore again in the famous stories of his meeting with the Queen of Sheba and his building of the Temple. A Muslim version tells how a dove whose job it was to stand with wings outspread before a certain window in Solomon's palace to keep out the fierce rays of the sun suddenly disappeared. Solomon was angry and vowed to kill it. But the dove returned to say that it had flown many many miles to a distant kingdom, the kingdom of Yemen, (identified with Sheba), where lived a queen named Bilkis, rich, powerful and wise, but who had not yet discovered the one, true God. Solomon resolves to try to convert the queen and her people, and so sends back an invitation to Jerusalem by the same bird. In the Jewish version of the story the bird is the hoopoe, Solomon's favourite messenger and confidant.

The hoopoe goes off with a host of other birds to the city of Kitor in the East, and their massed wings darken the sun above the queen's head. The queen takes the message from the hoopoe's wings, and resolves to accept the invitation saying that she will travel the seven-year journey to Jerusalem in only three.

The Muslim story tells how the queen brought with her as gifts many bars of silver and gold. Solomon anticipated her and made a road seven miles long leading up to Jerusalem and paved it with silver and gold bars. But he had judicially left gaps in the paving. When the Queen of Sheba's men arrived they noticed the gaps and were afraid, saying, 'the king will suspect us of stealing these bars'. So they filled in the gaps with the bars they had brought with them, and lo and behold! they had just the right number, not one more or less. This made them marvel at Solomon's great wisdom, and prepared them for the wonders they were to experience.

Both the Jewish and Muslim versions speak of the riddles that the queen posed Solomon. This is an expansion of the simple Biblical statement that 'she came to prove him with hard questions . . . And Solomon told her all her questions; there was not any thing hidden from the king which he told her not' (I Kings 10:1–3). More than twenty riddles are enumerated in the Jewish story alone. One that is common to both versions concerns the three thousand youths and three thousand maidens, 'who were born in the same year, in the same month, on the same day, in the same hour', all of equal stature, and wearing identical clothes. Solomon was asked to distinguish between the sexes. The Muslim Solomon watched them washing at a fountain, and he noticed that some allowed the water to fall on the backs of their hands, while others cupped their hands to collect the water. The first group were the boys and the second the girls. The Jewish Solomon devised a test. He ordered nuts and roasted ears of corn to be put before them. Those that seized them greedily were the boys. The ones with the more dainty manners were the girls.

It is curious that the Jewish legend unlike the Muslim does not expand on the subject of converting the queen. The source of this aspect of the story is in the Biblical account: 'The Queen of Sheba heard of the fame of Solomon because of the name of the Lord,' and then after he had solved the riddles she exclaims, 'Blessed be the Lord, thy God, who delighted in thee to set thee on the throne of Israel; because the Lord loved Israel for ever, therefore he made thee king, to do justice and righteousness' (I Kings 10:1; 9). Therefore the assumption is that she did recognise the God of Israel, although the Jewish tradition does not explicitly state it. Both religions however have a tradition that Solomon married the Queen of Sheba, and a Jewish legend has it that one of their sons was none other than Nebuchadnezzar, King of Babylon.

Solomon's Throne

One of the wonders which the Queen of Sheba came to marvel at was
Solomon's throne. It was but a pale imitation of the divine throne
itself in heaven, but it was resplendent enough nevertheless.

The throne is described in some detail in the Bible itself. 'The
king made a great throne of ivory, and overlaid it with the finest
gold. There were six steps to the throne, and the top of the throne
was round behind; and there were arms on either side by the place of
the seat, and two lions standing beside the arms. And twelve lions
stood there on the one side and on the other upon the six steps: there
was not the like made in any kingdom.' (I Kings 10:18–20.)

This account is elaborated in even greater detail in the legends.
Both to the left and the right on each of the six steps were a golden
lion and a golden eagle facing one another. In addition each step
carried a pair of different animals. On the first and lowest step stood
an ox and a lion; on the second a lamb and a wolf; on the third a
leopard and a goat; on the fourth an eagle and a peacock; on the fifth
a falcon and a cock; and on the sixth a hawk and a sparrow. All these
creatures were made of gold. One tradition has it that a demon went
up to heaven and took some of the sapphire pavement that lay below
the divine throne and brought it down to lay before Solomon. The
throne had a mechanical contrivance which led Solomon to his seat.
As soon as he put his foot on the lowest step the ox received him and
passed him to the animal on the step above, and so on up the six
steps until at the very top eagles raised him aloft and placed him on
the throne. Above Solomon's head flew a dove and in her beak a copy
of the Torah which she would place before the king so that 'he might
read therein day and night'.

This was Solomon's throne of judgment. Around it were seventy
thousand thrones for the sages, scholars, priests, Levites and princes
of Israel, and before it stood seventy thrones for the court of the
Sanhedrin. Immediately in front were two thrones, one for Gad, the
seer, and the other for Nathan, the prophet, and on Solomon's right
was a throne for his mother, Bathsheba.

As Solomon mounted the throne, heralds would remind him of
his responsibilities. At the first step he would hear one proclaim,
'He shall not multiply wives for himself'; at the second, 'He shall

not multiply horses for himself'; on the third, 'He shall not greatly multiply for himself gold and silver'; at the fourth, 'Thou shalt not pervert justice'; at the fifth, 'Thou shalt not be partial'; at the sixth, 'Thou shalt not take a bribe'; and as he reached the top, 'Know before whom thou standest.'

When the process of judgment began witnesses would approach with fear and trembling, terrified by the noise that the animals made: the ox lowed, the lion roared, the wolf howled, the lamb bleated, the leopard growled, the goat cried, the falcon shrieked, the peacock screamed, and the sparrow chirped; and the machinery of the throne itself began to rumble loudly. This prevented the witnesses from giving false evidence. (Jellinek, *Beth ha-Midrash V*, 34–9.)

The fate of the throne is something of a mystery. Rehoboam, Solomon's son, is supposed to have given it to Pharaoh as some kind of compensation for his widowed daughter. Sennacherib of Assyria captured it, but when he was defeated outside Jerusalem he had to surrender it to Hezekiah. Many years later it was again captured by Egypt. Pharaoh Necho tried to mount the steps, but he was injured by one of the lions, and limped ever after. The throne passed into the possession of Nebuchadnezzar, King of Babylon. He too suffered when he tried to climb the steps to the throne. Successive owners were the leaders of Persia, Greece and Rome, but of all these only Cyrus was allowed actually to sit upon it, this being his reward for allowing the Jewish exiles to return to Jerusalem.

Building the Temple

When Solomon set about constructing the Temple he was able to press into service all the demons and spirits, since every part of God's kingdom had to share in the construction of his earthly home.

The site of the Temple itself had already been acquired by Solomon's father, David, when he bought the threshing-floor of Araunah the Jebusite, and built an altar there (II Samuel 24:18 ff). But the site was confirmed to Solomon, when he heard a heavenly voice tell him to go one night to Mount Zion. There was a field there owned jointly by two brothers, one of whom was a bachelor and very poor, while the other was rich and had a large family. It was harvest-time and while Solomon was there he saw the poor brother come out secretly at night and take some of his own grain and add it to his brother's, thinking that his brother's need was greater because although he was richer he had a large family to support. Shortly afterwards the rich brother appeared and moved some of his grain in the opposite direction, saying that his poor brother's need was greater than his own, even though he did not have the burden of a large family. Solomon was so impressed by this demonstration of selflessness and brotherly love that he decided there and then that that should be the site of the Temple.

The participation of the spirits came about almost by accident. When the building operations had only just begun it was reported to Solomon that money and food belonging to one of his favourite attendants was being consistently stolen. This turned out on investigation to be the work of a malevolent spirit. Solomon was unable to apprehend the culprit, until he prayed to God, and the angel Michael appeared and gave him a special ring. While Solomon wore this ring he had power over all the demons, and could summon them to his bidding. Some of them were set to work to dig the foundations, others to melt down silver and gold, while Ornias the vampire spirit, who was the thief Solomon had been looking for, cut stones.

The Shamir

The actual blocks of stone used for the Temple itself had to be cut in a special way. The Torah stipulates that no cutting tool should be used in preparing the stone for the altar of the sanctuary. One tradition states that the Temple built itself, the stones coming out of the quarries of their own free will and placing themselves in serried ranks on the Temple site (*Zohar* I, 74a). But another, which we find in more than one source, tells us that Solomon used the marvellous shamir. What exactly the shamir was is open to question. The oldest sources do not define it, but the medieval authorities think of it as some kind of worm or insect which could bore through the hardest of minerals including diamond. Moses used it to engrave the names of the twelve tribes of Israel on the precious stones on the High Priest's breastplate.

But how was Solomon to acquire this wonderful creature? The spirits told him that they thought that Asmodai, the king of all the demons, knew where it was. Asmodai lived on a mountain where there was a well which provided him with his drinking water. Every day before he went up to heaven to participate in the discussions in the celestial academy he would place a heavy stone over the mouth of the well, and seal it. When he came back he would examine the seal to make sure that no one had tampered with the water. And then he would drink.

Solomon thought he would capture this Asmodai. So he sent his right-hand man, Benaiah, to fetch him, equipped with only a chain, a skin full of wine, some wool, and his special ring engraved with the divine name. When Benaiah reached the well he bored a hole in it from below, so that all the water drained away. He then plugged the hole with the wool. He drilled another hole from above into the well and filled the well with wine, being careful not to touch the seal. Benaiah then climbed a tree and awaited the demon-king's return. The unsuspecting Asmodai drew what he thought was water from the well. He was surprised by the different taste, but he liked it so much that he drank more than was good for him and fell ino a drunken stupor. Benaiah quickly came down from the tree and put the chain round his neck. Asmodai awoke and struggled but was quelled by the ring with the divine name, and was eventually brought before Solomon.

Solomon asked Asmodai the whereabouts of the shamir. 'God has entrusted it to the angel of the sea,' Asmodai replied, 'and the angel has in turn given it for safekeeping to the hoopoe. The hoopoe takes the shamir to mountains where man has never set foot and uses it to bore through the rocks. It then plants seeds there which grow, and make these deserted parts inhabitable.'

Solomon immediately sent one of his servants after the hoopoe, equipping him only with a sheet of glass. The man found the hoopoe's nest and laid the glass over it. When the hoopoe returned and found it could not get into its nest it flew away again to fetch the shamir from its secret hiding-place, so that it could eat its way through the glass. It had no sooner laid the shamir on the glass when the man gave a big shout, frightened the hoopoe away and seized the shamir. The poor bird was so upset at having broken its pledge to the angel of the sea that it took its own life. But the shamir was now in Solomon's possession, and he was able to use its skills in the construction of the Temple. (*Gittin* 68a–b.)

During the seven years that it took to build the Temple no workman died or was even injured, and all their tools and implements retained their pristine condition. But once the Temple was finished both men and equipment deteriorated rapidly so that they could not be used for constructing pagan shrines. The artisans' reward was preserved for them in the world to come.

Solomon Defeated

Solomon's encounter with Asmodai led to his temporary embarrassment. He taunted the demon saying that although he was king of the spirit-world he must be relatively powerless if he could be enchained by a mere mortal like Solomon. Asmodai thereupon told Solomon he would demonstrate his power if only he would lend him the magic ring. Solomon foolishly agreed. Asmodai immediately cast off his chains, picked up Solomon and threw him a thousand miles away, and pretended himself to be the king in Jerusalem.

Solomon was forced to wander the world for three years as a beggar, trying to convince the incredulous people that he was really the great and wise King Solomon. This humiliation served two purposes. It was, firstly, a punishment for the fact that Solomon had transgressed the divine command in the matter of wives, horses, and great wealth; and, secondly, it served to fulfil God's wish that Solomon should marry Naamah, the daughter of the King of Ammon, who was to prove to be the mother of King Rehoboam, and thus an ancestress of the Messiah. Solomon came to Ammon, and took employment in the royal kitchen. He exhibited such skill that he was soon promoted to be chief cook. It was in this capacity that he met the princess Naamah, and they fell in love. As soon as the king discovered this liaison he banished both of them from the palace. They wandered through desert lands until they came to a city by the sea-shore. Solomon bought a fish for the one meal they ate each day. As she was preparing it Naamah found a ring that had been swallowed by the fish. It was Solomon's own magic ring that Asmodai had thrown away into the sea.

With this ring on his finger Solomon transported himself back to Jerusalem, expelled Asmodai, and re-established himself as king with his new wife Naamah as his queen. (Jellinek, *Beth ha-Midrash* II, 86–87.)

The opposition that Solomon encountered to his marriage was paralleled according to another legend by his own opposition to his daughter's marriage. He learnt in a vision that she would fall in love with an extremely poor young man. Solomon was so intent on stopping their liaison that he shut her up in a tower which he had constructed in the Mediterranean Sea. As if this was not safe enough he had the tower guarded by seventy eunuchs. But 'many waters cannot quench love' as Solomon himself wrote. A poor young lad lost his way one cold night on the mainland not far from the tower. And he took shelter in the carcass of an ox which he found lying in a field. He was warm there, and he fell asleep. An enormous bird picked up the carcass with the youth still in it, and took it to the roof of the tower so that he could pick its bones. The young man was the princess's destined husband. She met him in the tower and after he had explained how he had found his way there she arranged for him to bathe and to put on new clothes. She was struck by his beauty, and also by his wisdom, and they fell in love. He married her according to Jewish law, writing the *ketubah*, the marriage contract, in his own blood, and inviting the angels Gabriel and Michael to be his witnesses while he recited the formula of betrothal.

When she became pregnant her guards decided that Solomon should be told. He was so impressed by his new son-in-law's wisdom and handsome bearing that he became reconciled to their marriage (*Tanhuma* ed-Buber, Introd., p. 136).

Solomon's Death

The Bible does not tell us the circumstances of Solomon's death. He simply 'slept with his fathers' (I Kings 11:43), and Jewish legend is also strangely silent on the subject. The Muslims, however, relate a fascinating story. Solomon had a foreboding that his death was near at hand; but the Temple had not yet been completed, and he knew that after his death the jinn whom he had pressed into service would immediately stop work on the Temple.

Every day in Solomon's garden a new tree would grow, and it was his habit to ask the tree its name and purpose. One day the new tree said, 'I shall be used for the destruction of the Temple. Make a staff out of me, and lean on me.' Solomon knew that his end was nigh.

He did as he was bidden, and went into the Temple, and leaned on the staff. He prayed that God would not let the jinn know of his death.

This prayer was granted. Solomon died crouched over his staff. Everyone who passed by, including the jinn, thought that he was deep in prayer, as was his wont, and they would not disturb him. Days, weeks, and months went by, and all this while a white ant gnawed its way into the staff and began eating it little by little from the inside. After a year had passed the staff collapsed into powder and Solomon fell, and the people and the jinn realised that he was dead. But by that time the Temple, Solomon's great masterpiece, stood finished in all its glory. (Rappoport III, 207–9.)

ELIJAH

ELIJAH IS one of the key figures in Jewish legend. It is not difficult to see how he became a focus of attention at all levels of religious consciousness, from that of the sublime mystic striving for a vision of the divine, to the popular imagination of an unlettered Jew who saw in Elijah a friend ready to help him in moments of distress. The image of Elijah assumed many forms and fulfilled many functions. But they all derived their efficacy from the powerful story of Elijah in the Bible itself.

Elijah in History

There he is firmly rooted in history, living as he did in the reigns of Ahab and Ahaziah, in the ninth century BCE. At the same time he displays characteristics which have an eternal quality. Indeed, he seems to span two worlds. He is involved in the sophisticated urban society of the court but he brings to that society the elemental religious passions of the wilderness. It is this paradoxical combination that gives the Elijah story its unique flavour.

He appears on the scene suddenly, without any preparation on the part of the writer, as if we are expected to know all about him from other sources, and he immediately establishes his authority. 'Elijah the Tishbite, of Tishbe in Gilead, said to Ahab: "I swear by the life of the Lord the God of Israel, whose servant I am, that there shall be neither dew nor rain these coming years unless I give the word"' (I Kings 17:1). He then disappears as swiftly as he came. He does not wait for Ahab's reaction. The story continues immediately: 'Then the word of the Lord came to him: "Leave this place and turn eastwards. . . ."' These opening words of the story set their seal on all subsequent accounts of Elijah and the part he plays in Jewish tradition. He appears suddenly. He speaks with authority. He is

imbued with mystery. And he is alone. This solitariness is
constantly reiterated in the Bible. 'The people of Israel have forsaken
thy covenant . . . I alone am left' (19:10, 14); 'I am the only prophet
of the Lord still left' (18:22). His contest with the four hundred and
fifty prophets of Baal emphasises his uniqueness. It is as if he carries
on his shoulders the whole weight of responsibility for God's
continued association with Israel. The choice that the people have to
make is presented in a stark and simple fashion: 'If the Lord is God,
follow him; but if Baal, then follow him' (18:21). The prophets of
Baal despite all their gyrations and self-mutilation cannot prevail
upon their god to appear in fire and consume the sacrifice of the
bullock that has been prepared. Elijah taunts them, and pointedly
stresses his superiority and that of his God by pouring water round
the altar, and then he prays 'at the hour of the regular sacrifice' – to
show that this was to be no exceptional occurrence – and 'the fire of
the Lord fell'. The people's response, 'The Lord, he is God; the Lord,
he is God' (18:39), is an absolute and uncompromising answer to
the choice with which they were faced, and it was later installed as
the great declaration of faith repeated seven times at the end of the
Day of Atonement service. In his great zeal on God's behalf Elijah
orders the slaughter of the priests of Baal. This passion recalls that of
Phinehas, son of Eleazar, who stopped a plague by transfixing with
his spear an Israelite and his Midianite paramour (Numbers 25:8).
Some rabbinic traditions went so far as to identify Elijah with
Phinehas.

In the two other major episodes of Elijah's life there are parallels
with Moses and Enoch. In Exodus Moses is accorded a partial
revelation of God. He is not permitted to see God's glory. But God
places him 'in a crevice of the rock', and as God's glory passes by he
is allowed to see only God's 'back' while his face 'shall not be seen'.
On the very same mountain, Horeb, Elijah too gains his most
intimate knowledge of the divine presence. 'The Lord was passing
by', and Elijah was in a cave, perhaps the very same 'cleft' which had
sheltered Moses. The revelation here, however, is not a sight but a
sound, the 'still, small voice'. This encounter with God on the
sacred mountain appears to be the climax of Elijah's mission,
because immediately thereafter, in the abrupt style with which we
have become accustomed in the Elijah narrative, he sets out to find a
successor: 'So he departed and found Elisha' (I Kings, 19:19).

The Ascent of Elijah

Elijah is soon to disappear from the scene. But he does not die. He, like Enoch, is simply 'taken'. In one of the most skilful literary passages in the whole Bible we are told how Elijah ascends to heaven. The author explains what is to happen in the simplest manner possible: 'The time came when the Lord would take Elijah up to heaven in a whirlwind' (II Kings 2:1). And then the reader is kept in suspense while Elijah and Elisha travel from Gilgal to Bethel, from Bethel to Jericho, and then across the Jordan which is miraculously parted by Elijah's cloak. Elisha asks for a double share of Elijah's spirit, and Elijah cryptically replies: 'If you see me taken from you, may your wish be granted; if you do not, it shall not be granted.' This puts the reader, or listener, on the alert, because he too wishes to 'see' Elijah taken. And it happens suddenly. Elijah's exit is as abrupt as his entry: 'They went on, talking as they went, and suddenly there appeared chariots of fire and horses of fire, which separated them one from the other, and Elijah was carried up in the whirlwind to heaven.' Elisha *did* see it. 'When Elisha saw it, he cried: "My father, my father, the chariots and the horsemen of Israel!" and he saw him no more' (2:12).

Reappearances of Elijah

The fact that Elijah's death is not recorded led to the conviction among later generations that he was still alive, and prompted many accounts of his reappearance and his continued support of the Jewish people both as individuals and as a corporate entity. It is said of him, for example, that he saved Persian Jewry from Haman, and that he protected from persecution the Jews of Bagdad in the tenth century, of Istanbul in the sixteenth, and of Cracow in the reign of Casimir IV. References to him in rabbinic literature abound, and most of these references concern the help that he extends to the poor and the pious. Elijah himself is credited with the dictum that 'God searched all the good qualities that he could give to Israel, and he found nothing better than poverty.' The source goes on to say: 'Hence the proverb: Poverty suits Israel as a red bridle suits a white horse' (*Hagigah* 9b).

Rabbi Akiva was very poor in his early years. He had married the daughter of a rich man against her father's wishes, and he could not support her in the manner to which she was accustomed. But Elijah showed them that their penury was purely comparative. One cold night Akiva could provide no more than some paltry straw for his wife's bed. Elijah appeared to them in disguise and cried out in despair, 'Good people, please give me a little straw for my wife. She has just been delivered of a child, and I have nothing at all for her to lie on.' Akiva and his wife responded positively, realising that their own plight was not so serious after all. (*Nedarim* 50a.)

Rabbi Akiva, of course, was one of the greatest of all scholars, and Elijah had a close relationship with many of them, sustaining them in their efforts to uphold the law, and answering their doubts.

'Rabbi Kahana earned a living by going from house to house selling osier baskets. Once a Roman lady tried to seduce him. He said to her, "Let me first go and prepare myself." He went up to the roof, and flung himself down. Elijah suddenly appeared and caught him, saying, "You made me travel one thousand miles to get here." Rabbi Kahana said, "It is only my poverty that led me to this." Elijah therefore gave him a potful of coins.' (*Kiddushin* 40a.)

Revealer of Mysteries

Many of the rabbis' theological problems related to reward and punishment and the after-life. Elijah was well placed to answer questions of this type, because he had actually visited heaven. There is indeed a tradition that he started life as the angel Sandalfon, and that his stay on earth recorded in the Bible was but a physical interruption in his spiritual existence.

'Rabbi Baroka used to go to the market at Lapet. One day Elijah appeared to him there, and Rabbi Baroka asked him, "Are any of the people here destined to share in the world to come?" Elijah answered, "None." Meanwhile a man arrived who wore black shoes and had no fringes on his garment. "This man," Elijah said, "will share in the world to come." Rabbi Baroka therefore called him over and asked him what he did for a living. "I am a jailer," the man replied, "and I keep the men and women separate. At night I place my own bed between the men and women to prevent the commission of any wrong." . . . Then two other men appeared on

the scene. "These two will also share in the world to come," said
Elijah. Rabbi Baroka asked them what they did. "We are merry-
makers. When we see someone sad we cheer him up. And when we
see two people quarrelling we try to make peace between them."'
(*Taanit* 22a.)

On one occasion Elijah was punished for revealing too many of the
celestial secrets. It was his habit to attend the house of study
presided over by the patriarch Rabbi Judah. One day he was late. He
excused himself by saying that that day was the New Moon, and
that therefore additional prayers had to be said in heaven.
'Furthermore, Abraham, Isaac and Jacob take a long time, because
they are not allowed to pray together. Each one prays individually in
succession. If they were permitted to pray together their prayer
would be irresistible. God would have to respond, and the Messiah
would come immediately.' Rabbi Judah asked whether there were
any on earth whose prayers were so powerful. Elijah said, 'The
prayers of Rabbi Hayyah and his sons.' Rabbi Judah declared a fast
straight away and invited Rabbi Hayyah and his sons to lead the
community in prayer. When they mentioned the word for wind, the
winds blew. When they prayed for rain, the rains fell. They were
coming amid mounting excitement to the prayer for the resurrection
of the dead. The heavens became alarmed, and it was obvious to
them that Elijah had said more than he should. He was therefore
punished with blows of fire. He changed into a bear and put the
congregation to flight. So prayer ceased and the resurrection has not
yet taken place. (*Baba Metsia* 85b.)

One of the major problems in the Biblical account of divine
justice involves the suffering of the children for the sins of the
fathers. In Jewish legend some mitigation of this difficulty is
provided by Elijah. 'In the world to come the children who die
because of the sins of their fathers will stand in the company of the
righteous, and their fathers in the company of the wicked, and they
will say to God: "We died because of our fathers' sins. Let our
fathers now come to us through our merits." God will say: "Your
fathers sinned after your death; their sins accuse them." Elijah will
come to their defence. He will tell the children: "Say to God,
Which is the greater the attribute of mercy or the attribute of
punishment? God will say, The attribute of mercy. You must then
say, If we died because of the sins of our fathers, even though the

attribute of mercy is greater, how much more should they now come over to us? God will say, You are right. They shall come over to you."*(Ecclesiastes Rabbah* IV, 1.)

Forerunner of the Messiah

Although this story does not expressly mention it, there is an implicit connection with *Malachi* 4:5, 'I will send you the prophet Elijah before the great and terrible day of the Lord comes. He will reconcile fathers to sons, and and sons to fathers.' This was naturally interpreted by the rabbis as a reference to the Messianic age. One of Elijah's roles is to be an embodiment, or at least the fore-runner of the Messiah. And he is often portrayed as communicating knowledge of the Messiah and the circumstances of his arrival.

One of the most famous of rabbinic stories concerning Elijah and the Messiah relates the conversation he had with Rabbi Joshua ben Levi. 'Rabbi Joshua ben Levi met Elijah at the mouth of the cave of Rabbi Simeon ben Yohai. . . . He asked him, "When will the Messiah come?" Elijah replied, "Go and ask him." "But where is he?" "At the gate of Rome." . . . Rabbi Joshua went and found him. . . . He said, "When is the Master coming?" He replied, "Today". . . . Rabbi Joshua returned to Elijah . . . and said, "He spoke falsely to me, because he said he would come today, and he has not come." Elijah said, "He meant, Today if you hearken to my voice [Psalm 115:7]."' (*Sanhedrin* 98a.)

At the end of time Elijah will come and solve every unresolved problem of Jewish law. Such an impasse is concluded in the *Talmud* with the Aramaic word *teku*, meaning 'let it stand', i.e. there is no answer. This word was interpreted as an abbreviation for 'the Tishbite will solve all doubts and perplexities'.

Some scholars connect Elijah's knowledge of the Messiah with the custom of preparing a special chair for him at the ceremony of circumcision. The Chair of Elijah is placed next to that of the *sandek* who holds the child. Elijah is symbolically present in the empty chair at every circumcision, because who is to know whether that particular baby boy is not to be the Messiah himself? Others maintain that Elijah is present in order to ward off evil spirits who might wish to attack the child when he is at his most vulnerable. In some Jewish communities women in labour put an amulet inscribed with Elijah's name beneath their pillow.

Elijah was associated in popular imagination specifically with the birth of prominent Jewish mystics. The founder of the Hasidic movement in the eighteenth century, Rabbi Israel ben Eliezer, the Baal Shem Tov, had his birth foretold by Elijah. The father, Rabbi Eliezer, was a most hospitable man. He used to have lookouts in the village who were asked to bring strangers to his house. One of these visitors was Elijah in disguise. He was so warmly welcomed by his host and so well treated that on his departure he revealed his true identity and told Eliezer that he would have a son who would 'enlighten the eyes of Israel' (*Maasiyot Peliot* 24–5).

The founder of the sixteenth century kabbalistic sect of Safed, Rabbi Isaac Luria, was circumcised on the eighth day after birth, as enjoined by Jewish law, but only after Elijah had himself appeared to his father. And story has it that the ceremony would have been postponed had not Elijah arrived to hold the child. After the ceremony Elijah handed the baby back to his father saying, 'Take your child. Take good care of him, for he will spread a brilliant light throughout the world' (*Shivhe ha-Ari*). Luria's disciple, Rabbi Hayyim Vital, wrote of his master: 'He was occupied only with the study of the Talmud . . . then Elijah appeared to him and advised him to withdraw into solitude . . . and so he sat in a house on the bank of the Nile, was seized by the holy spirit and Elijah constantly appeared to him and taught him the secrets of the Torah' (Wiener p. 83).

There are numerous accounts of how Jewish mystics experienced 'a revelation of Elijah' by which they were initiated into the celestial mysteries. The most revered figure in kabbalah, Rabbi Simeon ben Yohai, the reputed author of the *Zohar*, is said in the *Talmud* to have been instructed by Elijah in the mysteries of God and the universe during the thirteen years that he was in hiding from the Romans with his son in a cave. The personality of Elijah remains in the forefront of the Jewish mind through two rituals in addition to the ceremony of circumcision. The yearning for the coming of Elijah and the firm hope in the establishment thereby of God's kingdom are expressed every week at the end of the Sabbath, at the ceremony of Havdalah, when a conscious separation is made between the holy and the profane, between the Sabbath and the days of the week to come. Songs are sung recalling Elijah's miraculous deeds and his great zeal. One of the most popular has the refrain, 'The prophet Elijah, the Tishbite from Gilead, may he come to us soon with the son of David, the Messiah.' Rabbinic tradition has it that Elijah will not come on the Sabbath itself. He is therefore most likely to arrive at the conclusion of the Sabbath, when the Jewish world should be in its most observant and pious state. But perhaps the most striking of all rituals connected with Elijah occurs on the eve of Passover. At the special meal called the Seder a cup of wine is reserved for Elijah, and at a fixed moment in the proceedings 'the door is opened for Elijah'. This is a poignant moment in the service, because in medieval European communities Jews were often at the mercy of angry mobs, incensed by the Christian Easter story of the culpability of the Jews. The opening of the door was therefore not only an expression of hospitality characteristic of the Passover service but also a gesture of defiance towards the enemy and of trust in God that he would defend his people and indeed send Elijah at that moment to announce the coming of the Messiah. But does Elijah come? There is a Hasidic story of a pious Jew who asked his rabbi: 'For about forty years I have opened the door for Elijah every Seder night waiting for him to come, but he never does. What is the reason?' The rabbi answered: 'In your neighbourhood there lives a very poor family with many children. Call on the man and propose to him that you and your family celebrate the next Passover in his house, and for this purpose provide him and his whole family with everything necessary for the eight days of Passover. Then on the Seder night Elijah will certainly come.' The man did as the rabbi told him, but after Passover he came to the rabbi and claimed that again he had waited in vain to see Elijah. The rabbi answered: 'I know very well that Elijah came on the Seder night to the house of your poor neighbour. But of course you could not see him.' And the rabbi held a mirror before the face of the man and said: 'Look, this was Elijah's face that night.' (Wiener p. 139.)

ESTHER

THE BOOK of Esther is unlike any other book of the Bible. Both in style and in content it is redolent of the flavour of a tale from the *Arabian Nights*. The scene is set in a splendid palace, with a throne-room and many anterooms, full of precious silver and gold plate. There are banquets attended by hundreds of guests; revelry and romance. Beyond the palace itself are luxurious gardens, and then the magnificent Persian city of Shushan, and further afield still the one hundred and twenty-seven provinces over which the king, Ahasuerus, holds sway. There are plots and counter-plots, deaths on a massive scale and also great rejoicing. Moreover, there is an almost non-religious, if not irreligious, atmosphere in the book. The name of God does not occur once, and it is strange that in all the Jewish celebrations at the downfall of the arch-enemy, Haman, there are no songs or psalms of thanksgiving addressed to God. Nor do the Jews pray to him in their hour of distress.

Yet this is the book which provides the foundation for the festival of *Purim*, a happy, sometimes riotous occasion, when the Book, or more accurately Scroll, of Esther is read in the synagogue in a very carefree atmosphere. The mention of the name of the Jewish hero Mordecai is greeted with cheers, while that of Haman is marked by boos, jeers and the sounds of rattles. Fancy-dress parties and satirical plays are also presented at this time. The main, more 'normal' religious observance is to fulfil the instruction in the book itself: to send gifts to the poor. There can be no question, however, that the principle feeling at the festival is one of triumph over one's enemies. It is the only occasion in the Jewish calendar when the Jews are permitted to let themselves go and celebrate the downfall of their persecutors, for Haman is not simply a character in a story. He is a symbol of all tyrants, and unlike Pharaoh his animosity towards the

Jews is prompted by their uniqueness: 'There is a certain people scattered abroad . . . and their laws are diverse from those of every people' (Esther 3:8). The Second Targum (Aramaic midrash) of the book expands Haman's statement at great length, listing all the specifically religious activities of the Jewish people, and adding the unfounded and malicious accusations which Haman is presumed to make to the king: 'On the seventh day they observe their Sabbath; they go to the synagogues, read from their books, translate from the prophets, curse our king and government, and say, "This is the day on which God rested. May he grant us rest from the pagans" . . . On the fifteenth day [of Tishri] they celebrate the Festival of Sukkot. They cover their roofs with foliage. They go to our parks and cut down palm branches for the festival; they gather citrons and devastate the willows. . . . So they waste away the whole year with their nonsensical practices.'

In this way the Jewish tradition transmutes what is in effect a pseudo-historical tale into a symbolic representation of a recurring theme in Jewish historical experience.

There were, however, other aspects of the story that needed to be explained or expanded. The omission of the divine name was corrected by seeing in a phrase of Mordecai's a reference to the deity. He says to Esther 'Deliverance will come to the Jews from another place' (4:14). The word 'place' (ha-makom) is a common term in rabbinic parlance for God. The rabbis therefore saw no difficulty in maintaining that Mordecai here directly mentioned God.

They also had problems with the compromising situation in which Esther found herself. According to the story, she took part in a nationwide beauty contest. King Ahasuerus was to choose for his queen the most beautiful girl in his kingdom. Was it not a little undignified, not to say immoral, for a Jewish girl to submit herself to such a sensual physical examination? The answer that the *Talmud* (*Megillah* 13a) gives is that Esther had the beauty and grace of an old lady. She was, in fact, seventy-five years old, and it was her mature and sedate charm that impressed the king! Moreover, Esther was already married. Mordecai was not only her guardian, but also her husband. And she never, in fact, occupied the bed of Ahasuerus. God supplied a female spirit instead who looked exactly like her (*Zohar* III, 276a).

A traditional religious element is also added to the book by the midrash concerning the part played by the Jewish children in the salvation of the people. It was their persistent devotion to the study of Torah, under the watchful supervision of their teacher, Mordecai, that finally turned the tables on Haman. Haman wanted first to kill the children, and he found them in the school with Mordecai studying Torah. Their mothers came with food and drink, and tried to persuade the children, who had been fasting, to eat before they died. But the children refused. They handed their books to their teachers, saying, 'We had hoped to be rewarded with long life for studying the sacred Scriptures. But since we are not worthy, you must take back the books.' Their cries, added to those of the teachers and the mothers, reached God in heaven. He said, 'I can hear the voices of little lambs.' Moses said to God, 'They are not lambs, but young Jewish children crying. They have been fasting for three days, and are to be put to death tomorrow.' God's pity was moved, and he broke the seal on the decree of destruction, and Israel was saved (*Abba Gorion* 37–8).

Bibliography

Basic Texts

Bible. Traditional Hebrew Massoretic Text. English translation: *The Holy
Scriptures*, Philadelphia, 1917
Rabbinic commentaries on the Bible (e.g. Rashi, Ibn Ezra, etc., and
supercommentaries) in standard editions of Rabbinic Bibles
CHARLES, R.H. (ed.) *The Apocrypha and the Pseudepigrapha of the Old
Testament* in English, Oxford, 1913
GASTER, T.H. *The Scriptures of the Dead Sea Scrolls*, London, 1957
Mishnah. El Ha-Mekorot edition, Jerusalem, 1955. Trans. H. Danby,
Oxford, 1933
Babylonian Talmud. Torah La-Am edition, Jerusalem, 1961. Trans. ed. I.
Epstein, London, 1935–52
Jerusalem Talmud, Krotoschin, 1886
Midrash Rabbah, Warsaw, 1887–91. Trans. H. Freeman and M. Simon,
London, 1939
Zohar. Pardes edition, Jerusalem, 1960. Trans. H. Sperling and M.
Simon, London, 1931

Other Hebrew sources

Aggadat Bereshit, ed. S. Buber, Cracow, 1902
Alphabet of Ben Sira, ed. M. Steinschneider, Berlin, 1858
Beth ha-Midrash, ed. A. Jellinek, Leipzig, 1853–87
CARO, J. *Maggid Mesharim*, Jerusalem, 1967
DRESNITZ, S. *Shivhe ha-Ari*, Leghorn, 1790
Mekhilta de-Rabbi Yishmael, ed. with trans. J.Z. Lauterbach, Philadelphia,
1933–35
Midrash Abba Gorion in *Sifre de-Aggadeta*, ed. S. Buber, Wilna, 1887.
Midrash Aggadah, ed. S. Buber, Vienna, 1894
Midrash ha-Gadol, Jerusalem, 1947–75
Midrash Tanhuma, ed. S. Buber, Wilna, 1885.
Pesikta de-Rav Kahana, ed. B. Mandelbaum, New York, 1962. Trans.
W.G. Braude and I.J. Kapstein, Philadelphia and London, 1975

Pesikta Rabbati, ed. M. Friedmann, Vienna, 1880. Trans. W.G. Braude,
New Haven and London, 1968
Pirke de-Rabbi Eliezer, Warsaw, 1852. Trans. G. Friedlander, London,
1916
Sefer ha-Peliah, Korzec, 1784
Sefer ha-Yashar, ed. S.P. Rosenthal, Berlin, 1898
Sha-arei Yerushalayim, Warsaw, 1865
Sifre to Deuteronomy, ed. L. Finklestein, New York, 1961
Sifre to Numbers, ed. M. Friedmann, Vienna, 1862
SINGER, S. (ed.) *The Authorised Daily Prayer Book*, London, 1962
Targum Pseudo-Jonathan, ed. M. Ginsburger, Berlin, 1903

Supporting Literature
ANDERSON, G.K. *The legend of the wandering Jew*, Providence, 1965
BRONNER, L. *Biblical personalities and archaeology*, Jerusalem, 1974
CASSUTO, U. *The Goddess Anath. Canaanite epics of the patriarchal age*,
Jerusalem, 1971
CROSS, F.M. *Canaanite myth and Hebrew epic*, Cambridge, Mass., 1973
DAICHES, D. *Moses. Man in the wilderness*, London, 1975
Epic of Gilgamesh, The, trans. N. Sandars, Harmondsworth, 1970
GASTER, M. *The Exempla of the Rabbis*, London, 1924
GASTER, M. *Ma'aseh Book. Book of Jewish tales and legends*, 2 vol
Philadelphia, 1934
GASTER, M. *Studies and texts in folklore, magic,* etc., 3 vol. London,
1925–28. Reprinted 1971, with a Prolegomenon by T.H. Gaster
GASTER, T.H. *Myth, legend and custom in the Old Testament*, London,
1969
GASTER, T.H. *Thespis. Ritual, myth and drama in the Ancient Near East*,
New York, 1950
GIBSON, J.C.L. *Canaanite myths and legends*, Edinburgh, 1978
GINZBERG, L. *The legends of the Jews*, 7 vol. Philadelphia, 1947. (Cited as
'Ginzberg'.) A one-volume edition, with an introduction by S. Spiegel,
Philadelphia, 1956
GINZBERG, L. *On Jewish law and lore*, Philadelphia, 1955
HANAUER, J.E. *Folklore of the Holy Land, Moslem, Christian and Jewish*,
London, 1935
HEIDEL, A. *The Babylonian Genesis*, 2nd edn. Chicago, London, 1963
HEIDEL, A. *The Gilgamesh Epic and Old Testament parallels*, Chicago,
1946
HEINEMANN, J. and NOY, D. *Studies in Aggadah and folk-literature*,
Jerusalem, 1971. *Scripta Hierosolymitana*, Vol. 22
HOOKE, S.H. *Middle Eastern Mythology*, Harmondsworth, 1963
JACOBSEN, T. *The Sumerian King List*, Chicago, 1939. *Oriental Institute of
the University of Chicago, Assyrological Studies*, 11

JAMES, F. *Personalities of the Old Testament*, New York, London, 1939
KING, L.W. *Legends of Babylon and Egypt in relation to Hebrew tradition*, London, 1918. (The Schweich Lectures, 1916)
LANGDON, S.H. *The Babylonian Epic of Creation*, Oxford, 1923
LICHT, J. *Storytelling in the Bible*, Jerusalem, 1978
MEYOUHAS, J. *Bible tales in Arab folklore*, London, 1928
MONTEFIORE, C.G. and LOEWE, H. *A Rabbinic anthology*, London, 1938
PATAI, R. *Man and temple in ancient Jewish myth and ritual*, London, 1947
PRITCHARD, J.B. *Ancient Near Eastern texts relating to the Old Testament*, Princeton, 1955
PRITCHARD, J.B. *Solomon and Sheba*, London, 1974
RANELAGH, E.L. *The past we share. The Near Eastern ancestry of Western folk-literature*, London, 1979
RAPHAEL, C. *A feast of history. The drama of Passover through the ages*, London, 1972
RAPPOPORT, A.S. *The folklore of the Jews*, London, 1937.
RAPPOPORT, A.S. *Myths and legends of ancient Israel*, London, 1928. (Cited as 'Rappoport') Revised Ed. with an Introduction by R. Patai, New York, 1966
SCHRIRE, T. *Hebrew amulets*, London, 1966
SCHWARZBAUM, H. *Studies in Jewish and world folklore*, Berlin, 1968
SEYMOUR, ST.J.D. *Tales of King Solomon*, London, 1924
SPEISER, E.A. (ed.) *Genesis*, New York, 1964 (*The Anchor Bible*)
TRACHTENBERG, J. *Jewish Magic and superstition*, New York, 1939
VAN SETERS, J. *Abraham in history and tradition*, New Haven, London, 1975
VILNAY, Z. *Legends of Galilee, Jordan and Sinai*, Philadelphia, 1978
VILNAY, Z. *Legends of Jerusalem*, Philadelphia, 1973
VILNAY, Z. *Legends of Judea and Samaria*, Philadelphia, 1975
WIENER, A. *The Prophet Elijah in the development of Judaism*, London, 1978
YARDEN, L. *The tree of light. A study of the Menorah*, Cornell, 1971

Index

Page numbers in italics refer to illustrations

Acknowledgements

Photographs
Biblioteca Ambrosiana, Milan 124; Bibliothèque Nationale, Paris 118; British Library, London 49, 50, 53 top, 53 bottom, 54 bottom, 115, 117, 123; British Museum, London 51 top; Brotherton Library, University of Leeds 60; Chester Beatty Library, Dublin 55; Encyclopaedia Judaica, Jerusalem 52, 56, 61, 121 bottom; Encyclopaedia Judaica – Itzhack Amit 127; Encyclopaedia Judaica – *Jewish Observer* 125; Encyclopaedia Judaica – Spiral Press 116; Hamlyn Group – John Webb 121 top; The Hashemite Kingdom of Jordan Department of Antiquities, Amman 51 bottom; Hebrew Union College, Skirball Museum, Los Angeles, California 59; Hessische Landes- und Hochschulbibliothek, Darmstadt 62; Israel Museum, Jerusalem 64, 126; Jewish Museum, New York 57; Jewish National and University Library, Jerusalem 114, 120; John Rylands Library, Manchester 63; Staatsbibliothek Preußsischer Kulturbesitz, Berlin 122, 128; Warburg Institute, London 54 top; Sir Isaac and Lady Wolfson Museum, Hechal Shlomo, Jerusalem 113; Yale University Art Gallery, New Haven, Connecticut 119.

The illustration on page 116 is from *Ecclesiastes, or the Preacher*, Spiral Press, New York, 1965.